Rediscovering Jacob Riis

Rediscovering Jacob Riis

*Exposure Journalism and Photography
in Turn-of-the-Century New York*

. . . .

Bonnie Yochelson & Daniel Czitrom

THE NEW PRESS

NEW YORK
LONDON

Requests for permission to reproduce selections from this book should be mailed to:
Permissions Department, The New Press, 38 Greene Street, New York, NY 10013.

Published in the United States by The New Press, New York, 2007
Distributed by W. W. Norton & Company, Inc., New York

LIBRARY OF CONGRESS CATALOGING-IN-PUBLICATION DATA
Yochelson, Bonnie.
Rediscovering Jacob Riis : exposure journalism and photography in
turn-of-the-century New York / Bonnie Yochelson and Daniel Czitrom.
p. cm.
Includes bibliographical references and index.
ISBN 978-1-59558-199-0
1. Documentary photography—New York (State)—New York—History—19th
century. 2. Crime and the press—New York (State)—New York—History—19th
century. 3. New York (N.Y.)—Social life and customs—19th
century—Pictorial works. 4. Riis, Jacob A. (Jacob August), 1849–1914. I.
Riis, Jacob A. (Jacob August), 1849–1914. II. Czitrom, Daniel J., 1951-
III. Title.
TR820.5.Y645 2008
770.9747'1—dc22   2007035015

The New Press was established in 1990 as a not-for-profit alternative to the large,
commercial publishing houses currently dominating the book publishing industry.
The New Press operates in the public interest rather than for private gain, and is
committed to publishing, in innovative ways, works of educational, cultural, and
community value that are often deemed insufficiently profitable.

www.thenewpress.com

Book design by Lovedog Studio

This book was set in Electra

Printed in the United States of America

2 4 6 8 9 7 5 3 1

For Meryl
And for Betty and Molly
A kind's khokhme iz oykh khokhme

D.C.
Cherry Street, New York City

B.Y.

Contents

Acknowledgments

This book grew out of a 1994 Preservation and Access Grant from the National Endowment for the Humanities (NEH) for the Jacob A. Riis Collection at the Museum of the City of New York. The museum's most historically significant collection of photographs, the Riis Collection poses unique interpretative problems: to make it properly accessible, NEH supported the creation of a database, vintage-material prints from Riis's negatives, and color transparencies from his lantern slides. That project was supervised by Bonnie Yochelson, formerly the museum's Curator of Prints and Photographs. She would like to thank Chicago Albumen Works; Housatonic, Massachusetts, which expertly created the "new" Riis prints and transparencies; and Peter Simmons, then head of Collections Access, who established the Riis database. Other museum staff who deserve grateful thanks are Eileen Kennedy Morales, former head of Collections Access; Bob Shamis, former

Curator of Prints and Photographs; Marguerite Lavin, former head of Rights and Reproductions; and Rick Beard, former deputy director of Programs and Collections, who introduced this study's co-authors.

A second NEH grant (1997–2000) in Collaborative Research funded our research on Jacob Riis, his work, and his world. The grant allowed us to hire Kevin P. Murphy, then a New York University doctoral student, who provided much appreciated assistance reviewing Riis's voluminous papers, and who gave us access to his valuable unpublished paper on Riis's posthumous reputation; and Lone Blecher of New York City, who translated Riis's 1870–71 pocket diaries (New York Public Library) and provided us with summaries of his Danish journalism (Library of Congress). We offer grateful thanks to them both.

For additional archival research, we wish to thank Holly Hinman, New-York Historical Society; Jean Ashton, Columbia University Rare Books and Manuscripts; Nancy Cataldi, Richmond Hill Historical Society; Victor Rener, Children's Aid Society; and Lorinda Klein, Bellevue Hospital. We received valuable research help as well from Jennifer Cote and Sara E. Rzeszutek. For an introduction to the still little-studied world of lantern slides, special thanks to Terry Borton, East Haddam, Connecticut; Jack Judson, San Antonio, Texas; and Tom Rall, Arlington, Virginia.

We are also pleased to thank Donal O'Shea, dean of faculty at Mount Holyoke College, who provided crucial material and moral support for the publication of this book. Also at Mount Holyoke, we received important production help from Linda Callahan, Slide Curator of the Art Library, and James Gehrt, Digitization Center coordinator.

We thank Mike Wallace and Suzanne Wasserman at the Gotham Center for New York History, Graduate Center of the City University of New York, and Christopher Benfey and Karen Remmler at the Weissmann Center for Leadership and the Liberal Arts, Mount Holyoke College, for inviting us to make public presentations of our work in its early stages.

Jacob A. Riis ca. 1900, gelatin silver print,
Museum of the City of New York.

Introduction

When Jacob Augustus Riis died on May 25, 1914, at the age of sixty-five, he was a beloved public figure. *How the Other Half Lives*, his 1890 call-to-conscience for housing reform, had been a bestseller and was still in print. *The Making of an American*, his popular 1901 autobiography, which told the heartwarming story of his rise from penniless immigrant to confidant of President Theodore Roosevelt, had made him a celebrity. His nationwide lecture tours and steady stream of magazine stories had kept his message in public view. Nearly a century later, Riis maintains a stubbornly persistent hold on the American imagination. The twin themes of his writing—urban poverty and the Americanization of the immigrant—are as relevant today as in his time. The recovery in the 1940s of Riis's original photographs—images of decrepit rear tenements, "black-and-tan dives," newsboys, and "little mothers," which constitute a unique pictorial record of New York's late-nineteenth-century slums—added another dimension to his fame. Indeed, images such as "Bandit's Roost," which was reenacted in the 2002 Hollywood film *Gangs of New York*, have become emblems of urban poverty.

Our goal in this book is to rediscover Jacob Riis, whose motives and accomplishments have been often distorted by his advocates and detractors. The project grew out of a Collaborative Research Grant from the National Endowment for the Humanities (NEH), and we have tried to remain true to the spirit of interdisciplinary inquiry. We bring to bear our respective disciplines—history and art history—to establish a foundation for a new assessment of Riis's career. The book's two essays are arranged chronologically. Daniel Czitrom's "Jacob Riis's New York" begins with Riis's 1870 arrival in the United States and concludes with the 1890 publication of *How the Other Half Lives*. It situates Riis within the gritty specifics of Gilded Age New York, tracing his complex relations with the city's tenement neighborhoods, its new immigrants, its fiercely competitive journalism, its evangelical reformers, its labor movement, and its political machines. Drawing upon Lone Blecher's new translation from the Danish of Riis's pocket diaries of 1871–72 and her summaries of Riis's newspaper articles for Danish newspapers, Czitrom's essay offers the first detailed discussion of his journalism and his embrace of the housing reform cause.

Bonnie Yochelson's "Jacob A. Riis, Photographer 'After a Fashion'" begins with Riis's first lantern slide lecture in 1888 and concludes with his death in 1914. Building upon a prior NEH-funded access and preservation project of the Jacob A. Riis Collection at the Museum of the City of New York, Yochelson presents the first thorough study of Riis's photographs: resolving dating and attribution problems, characterizing his photographic practice, and assessing the influence of his photographs at a time of rapid technological change in the publishing industry.

Despite differences in approach and methodology, we share a common view of Riis's strengths and weaknesses. His most enduring legacy remains the written descriptions, photographs, and analysis of the conditions in which the majority of New Yorkers lived in the late nineteenth century. The new immigrants of the tenements—Italians, Jews, Bohemians, Chinese, Slavs, and "low Irish"—threatened the political stability of the city and the nation. The explosive mixture of grinding poverty, sweatshops, and mass immigration, the growing power of urban Democratic political machines, the declining influence of Protestant evangelical churches, the persistence of life-threatening public health conditions, the increase in child labor and juvenile crime, the "murder of the home"—all these were passionately portrayed in his "Studies Among the Tenements of New York," the subtitle of *How the Other Half Lives*.

In that first book, Riis employed every means he could muster to arouse his readers: curiosity, humor, shock, fear, guilt, and faith. His passion ignited his audience, but his message was not truly incendiary. A deeply contradictory figure, Riis was a conservative activist and a skillful entertainer who presented controversial ideas in a compelling but ultimately comforting manner. His social scientific method of careful observation and deployment of statistics and photographs would become hallmarks of the Progressive movement,

yet his writings hark back to several nineteenth-century literary traditions, including police journalism, Protestant charity writing, the
"sunshine and shadow" guidebooks to "the secrets of the great city,"
and the tales of Horatio Alger. His disturbing photographs were
safely embedded in Christian sermons. It was precisely Riis's ability
to straddle the old and the new that won the confidence of his audiences and secured his success.

Riis's reputation has endured many twists and turns over the past
century.[1] Progressive-era reformers saw him primarily through the
lens of his housing reform activism. In their classic 1903 study *The
Tenement House Problem*, the first comprehensive history of New
York housing and the campaigns to improve it, Robert W. DeForest
and Lawrence Veiller lauded Riis's work as having "done more to
educate the general public on the question than the writings of any
other person."[2] But even by 1914, when Theodore Roosevelt eulo-
gized him as "the ideal American citizen,"[3] a younger generation
of Progressive reformers considered him old-fashioned, rejecting
his faith in Christian charity and his distrust of government. Not
until the 1930s did Riis reemerge as a powerful source of inspiration for New Deal reformers. Secretary of Labor Frances Perkins
and New York Mayor Fiorello La Guardia, for example, both considered *How the Other Half Lives* a formative influence. For their
generation, Riis was the "great emancipator of the slums,"[4] important enough to warrant a full-scale biography by sociologist Louise
Ware.[5] Overlooking Riis's Republican politics and his faith in
Christian philanthropy as the solvent for urban problems, the New

Dealers commemorated him by placing his name on large-scale government-funded projects, such as Jacob Riis Park in Brooklyn (1937) and the Jacob Riis Houses in lower Manhattan (1949). On the centennial of Riis's birth in 1949, Robert Moses, who directed New York's massive urban renewal projects, claimed Riis as his forebear in a *New York Times Magazine* article.[6]

The Moses article was illustrated with photographs by Riis, which had only recently been recovered. In 1887, Riis had commissioned a group of photographs of the slums to illustrate a lecture that became the nucleus of *How the Other Half Lives.* Shortly thereafter, he began taking his own photographs, which he used in lectures, articles, and books throughout his career. Riis, however, did not value these photographs independent of his talks and writings and therefore did not prepare them, as he did his papers, for donation to libraries. Thanks to the detective work of photographer Alexander Alland, Riis's negatives and lantern slides were recovered from the attic of his house, and in 1947 the Museum of the City of New York presented an exhibition, "The Battle of the Slum," which featured fifty modern prints by Alland from Riis's negatives. In his seminal *History of Photography* published the next year, Beaumont Newhall established a lineage for social documentary photography, which began with Riis and led to Lewis Hine and Dorothea Lange.[7]

In noting that the subject of Riis's photographs was "no longer topical," Newhall expressed the optimism of the postwar economic recovery. By the 1960s, however, urban poverty had reemerged as a major public concern, inspiring renewed interest in the history of reform and in Riis. In the following decade, numerous reprints of Riis's books and three Riis biographies were published.[8] The authors and editors of these volumes found in Riis an affirmation of their belief that the "culture of poverty" was the result of a degraded environment, not defective character. They dismissed Riis's reliance on crude racial stereotypes, with which he peppered the text of *How the Other Half Lives,* as "the prejudices of his day."[9]

Most of these books were published with few if any illustrations, but as interest in fine art photography grew in the 1970s, two books that were extensively illustrated—the Dover reprint of *How the Other Half Lives* and Alland's biography—broadened Riis's reputation as a revolutionary photographer who initiated the social documentary tradition. Riis's supporters began to split into two largely autonomous camps: historians and social scientists who focused on his prose with little concern for his images, and the photography community, which lauded his images with only passing interest in his texts. In the 1980s, the growth of cultural studies fostered consideration of Riis's images and texts in tandem, and his slide lectures, often musically accompanied, were accurately characterized as popular entertainment. These critics and scholars shared a disillusionment with liberalism and a deep-seated skepticism about the "heroes" of liberal reform. For them, Riis's "reform" efforts strengthened barriers of class and race, prime examples of cultural surveillance in the service of social control.[10]

In the writings and lectures that followed *How the Other Half Lives* Riis stayed on message. But the racial stereotypes faded in favor of anecdotes about individuals, and his photographs also became more personal, with "flashlight" exposures giving way to portraits that evolved naturally out of interviews. Otherwise, the later books and articles are numbingly repetitive. Indeed, by the late 1890s, many of Riis's innovations, such as tenement-life storytelling and photographic illustration, became commonplace, and a change in sensibility occurred that left Riis behind. The shift can be seen, for example, in Stephen Crane's *Maggie, A Girl of the Streets* (1893), which scandalized the public not because of its subject matter but for its utter lack of moral uplift; or in Lincoln Steffens's *The Shame of the Cities* (1904), which employed a streetwise, cynical tone to expose government corruption. Steffens, who warmly regarded "Jake" Riis as a mentor, wrote about politics and crime with a clinical detachment that was entirely foreign to Riis.

Although his innovations quickly became commonplace, Riis posed a series of urgent, often implicit, questions to himself and his readers, which remain surprisingly apt today: What is the structural relationship between persistent poverty and new immigrants? If different "races" and nationalities possess inherent moral and cultural characteristics, how can that be reconciled with the American creed of individualism? How does environment shape "character"? What are the proper roles of government, private philanthropy, and religion in reform efforts? How important is spectacle and entertainment in rousing the public conscience?

While the Manhattan slum neighborhoods that Riis documented have been transformed into fabulously lucrative real estate, his work still resonates on a global level. The 2003 United Nations report on *The Challenge of Slums* presents a grim picture of a planet where more than 900 million people, nearly a third of the world's urban population, live in slums. That figure may reach a staggering 2 billion by 2030. The report summarizes the situation in twenty-nine city case studies with an urgency that echoes Riis: "Slums are distinguished by the poor quality of housing, the poverty of the inhabitants, the lack of public and private services and the poor integration of the inhabitants into the broader community and its opportunities. . . . Slum dwellers have more health problems, less access to education, social services and employment, and most have very low incomes."[11] In *Rediscovering Jacob Riis* we offer a fresh look at a journalist, reformer, and photographer whose world is long gone, but whose probing imagination, moral passion, and intellectual contradictions are as imperative as ever.

1

Jacob Riis's New York

. . . .

Daniel Czitrom

In the great "dumb-bell" tenements, in the rickety old frame buildings, in the damp, unwholesome cellars, on the sidewalks and in the gutters reeking of filth and garbage, is a seething mass of humanity, so ignorant, so vicious, so depraved that they hardly seem to belong to our species. Men and women; yet living, not like animals, but like vermin!

—Allan Forman, *American Magazine* (1888)

I miss all those ratty little wooden tenements, born with the smell of damp in which there grew up how many school teachers, city accountants, rabbis, cancer specialists, functionaries of the revolution, and strong-arm men for Murder, Inc.

—Alfred Kazin, *A Walker in the City* (1951)

The Making of a Journalist

The essentials of Jacob Riis's biography are well known, and indeed his life story long ago took its place beside other classic narratives of American immigration and assimilation. This was surely part of why Theodore Roosevelt famously referred to him as "the best American I ever knew." He was born in 1849, the third of fourteen children, and raised in the rural northern Danish town of Ribe. Riis's schoolmaster father, who also wrote for the local newspaper, had hoped his boy would pursue a literary career, but Jacob was a diffident student at best. He had no use for Latin or mathematics, but he did enjoy learning English, largely through reading the novels of Charles Dickens and James Fenimore Cooper. The teenage Riis traveled to Copenhagen where he lived for four years while learning the carpentry trade. He returned to Ribe in 1868, a nineteen-year-old member of the carpenters' guild, but he was deeply discouraged by the lack of work in the depressed rural districts of Denmark. His childhood sweetheart Elisabeth turned down his marriage proposal, in part because her prosperous, cotton mill–owning father thought a journeyman carpenter beneath his daughter's station. Thus both economic and personal motives shaped Riis's decision to immigrate to America. When he landed at New York's Castle Garden in June 1870, he brought with him very little cash, but he possessed other valuables that gave him advantages over most other immigrants of the day: a skilled trade, some knowledge of English, a burning ambition to succeed.[1]

Riis's first five years in the United States were extremely difficult. His autobiography recounts the life of an itinerant workingman, tramping across New Jersey, New York State, and the Midwest, including stints in lumber mills, shipyards, furniture factories, ice houses, and peddling books and flat irons. Riis's diary from this period, recently translated from the Danish, gives us a more emotionally nuanced picture of the young immigrant. In addition to the gnawing poverty and difficulties securing regular work, Riis suffered from severe homesickness and lovesickness. Daydreams of his parents and his unrequited love for Elisabeth brought on regular fits of deep depression. A long entry written on New Year's Eve, 1871, found Riis deeply depressed, wrestling with his religious faith, fearing that he would never see his parents again, and pining for his lost love, who had stopped writing:

The story of the year! O, God, it seems to me that I might sing on this last evening of the year:

"I have wandered about aimlessly.

Life's pearls I scattered like sand.

I have spent my hope and my faith and my peace,

And now I stand on the edge of the abyss."

God, please let not this be my mood next New Year's Eve; Give me peace, give me patience and trust in you during the difficult days ahead . . . Say whatever you will, the rest of you, She alone, Elisabeth is my only ideal, the ultimate perfection. Everything that a woman can ever mean in my eyes—and slander cannot touch her and never will, as long as I can lift a hand![2]

In this period Riis's experiences were representative of a large fraction of the American working class—economically insecure, full of doubt for the future, and, particularly in the wake of the 1873 depression, increasingly itinerant. He gave little attention to politics, save for the occasional denunciation of radicals. While working in a Buffalo shipyard he described how "the other day an international (socialist) babbler came up to our ship during the lunch break and attempted to fill the workers' ears with communism, but to the hilarity of everyone, I took him on and thoroughly ran down the internationals so he finally chose to make a sad retreat with all his fine intentions and hopes stranded. If ever such a gathering were to take place here in Buffalo, I really do believe that I would get up and speak, for the first time in English, against this crazy idea, which I hate. Well, I think people in this country are much too enlightened to buy such nonsense." The ideal or practice of class solidarity, either in unions or in politics, held no attraction for Riis. Nor would they ever, although he would later regularly invoke these early hard times as a source of his sympathy for working people.[3]

The diary also reveals Riis to have been uncomfortable with the working-class amusements enjoyed by his friends. He rued the $4 expense of a Christmas Day jaunt along Main Street in Jamestown, New York, "visiting on the way every saloon and public house, we enjoyed ourselves well and jovially . . . and drank until 2 o'clock and then back home to bed. All in all it might have been done in a somewhat more decent manner, considering it was a holiday!" After "having once witnessed American theater"—probably the popular burlesque spectacle *The Black Crook*—he wrote, "no earthly power will ever drag me along to anything like this phantasmagoria since it is all alike. The scenery was gorgeous, very fine costumes, sufficient female beauty to look at, exposed and not exposed, there was—Oh, I thought, if only we had a few of the well-known Danish ballet dancers in the government here, they would quickly gain another concept of 'The limitations for propriety in the theater.' . . . God have mercy! I never thought or dreamed of anything like it. I should think not!, now nothing can surprise me anymore."[4]

Uninterested in collective action and uneasy with the plebian pleasures of working-class culture, Riis instead pondered schemes for individual self-improvement, including writing newspaper articles for the Danish press (there were no takers) and taking a course in telegraphy (which he eventually did). The diary meticulously records his living expenses, wages, travels, and debts, along with his restlessness and the frequent bouts of despair that he believed might be the sign of a "dangerous nervous condition." Riis's diary also embodied the old Protestant tradition of examining the progess of the soul and looking to faith as a bulwark against laziness, wasted time, lack of direction—a harbinger of the piety and steely sense of purpose evident in the later writings. In these bleak early years Riis looked to God for help in fighting lethargy, sorrow, anguish, and "dark memories": "If these memories were always to be the master of me, I'd never amount to anything other than a layabout and a misanthrope; the shining hope for good times and happiness yet again, is penetrating, slowly but surely; if only it would finally be victorious and reach its goal."[5]

In the fall of 1873 Riis moved to East 30th Street in Manhattan, where he studied telegraphy and made his first forays into the newspaper world. He landed a $10-a-week job as a reporter for the New York News Association, which published his reports of city events in subscribing newspapers. By the spring of 1874 he had left for a reporting job with the *South Brooklyn News,* a small Democratic weekly that soon promoted him to editor. Riis made the paper a commercial success by adding crusading editorials and a lively gossip column to the partisan political stories, and early in 1875 he bought the paper. He had found his calling, and confided in his diary, "I really do think that journalism comes easy for me. At least, I've been successful in everything I touch in that field."[6] That same year he learned that Elisabeth's fiancé had died, and after resuming his courtship via mail, he sold the paper and used the profits to sail back to Denmark to marry her. They returned to Brooklyn in the summer of 1876, whereupon Riis resumed his editorship of the *South Brooklyn News*.

But a dispute with the owners led him to quit and briefly take up the advertising trade and, crucially, gain his first experience with photography. He bought his first stereopticon, or "magic lantern," and traveled that fall around towns and villages on Long Island, "giving open-air exhibitions in which the 'ads' of Brooklyn merchants were cunningly interlarded with very beautiful colored views, of which I had a fine collection. When the season was too far advanced to allow of this, I established myself in a window at Myrtle Avenue and Fulton Street and appealed to the city crowds with my pictures." Along with a partner Riis tried expanding this business by traveling through upstate New York towns, but they were unsuccessful. In the fall of 1877 he returned to New York and, after several rejections from city papers, he finally managed to land a staff position as a police reporter on the *New York Tribune*, where he remained until 1890. Many of his pieces would be routinely reprinted in other New York papers as part of the *Tribune*'s membership agreement with the Associated Press.[7]

Thus by 1877 the various uncertainties in Riis's life had been resolved. Settled in Brooklyn and working in Manhattan, he found his vocation, his wife, and his religion all at more or less the same time. In later years Riis recalled that his early forays into journalism occurred simultaneously with his conversion to Methodism. As he told it, he was so moved by the fiery eloquence of a local preacher that Riis offered to abandon his job at the *South Brooklyn News* to take up preaching himself. But the minister discouraged him: " 'We have preachers enough. What the world needs is consecrated pens.' Then and there I consecrated mine. I wish I could honestly say that it has always come up to the high ideal set it then. I can say, though, that it has ever striven toward it, and that scarce a day has passed since that I have not thought of the charge then laid upon it and upon me." Journalism would provide the outlet for both his reforming instincts—what he called "a reporter's public function"—as well as his own very competitive nature, "the only reknown I have ever coveted or cared to have, that of being the 'boss reporter' in Mulberry Street."[8]

Like nearly all reporters of his day, Riis struggled to make a living, which was why he pursued syndicated and freelance work even after joining the staff of the *Tribune*. Less well known than Riis's police reporting is the very different sort of journalism that he practiced simultaneously, one that today might be labeled feature writing. Much of this was composed in Danish and published in Riis's home country, and some found its way, through syndication, into American newspapers halfway across the continent. These articles focused less on New York doings and more on national politics, personality profiles, and scandals among the social elite. In pursuing both New York–centered police reporting and this more general sort of feature writing, Riis made himself proficient in two different journalistic styles, which melded into a hybrid that combined a debunking tone with his sharp commercial instincts. In short, through these twin journalistic experiences, Riis developed the critical themes and distinctive voice that would distinguish *How the Other Half Lives* and his later books.

From the Mulberry Street office, just across the street from police headquarters, Riis developed his lifelong reportorial encounter with New York's underside. His autobiography stressed what became known as the "human interest" aspect of the work. Riis defined the job as "the one who gathers and handles all the news that means trouble to some one: the murders, fires, suicides, robberies, and all that sort, before it gets into court." He sought to give meaning to it all as "a great human drama in which these things are the acts that mean grief, suffering, revenge upon somebody, loss or gain." The reporter's task, he argued, was to "portray it that we can all see its meaning, or at all events catch the human drift of it, not merely the foulness and the reek of blood." Indeed Gilded Age police work meant a great deal more than the prevention and solving of crimes [*Figures 1.1, 1.2*]. Policemen of the day were very visible public agents, particularly for the poor, the recent immigrants, and the city's huge "floating" population. They routinely provided lodging and sometimes food for the indigent, helped lost children find their parents, aided accident victims, transported the sick to hospitals, stopped runaway horses, fished unidentified bodies out of the harbor, and removed dead animals from the streets. To be sure, in addition to social welfare functions, police also engaged in repressive social control of "the dangerous classes" through the

FIGURE 1.1
"Familiar Incidents
in the Life of a New
York Policeman,"
from Augustin
Costello, *Our Police
Protectors* (1885).

power of arrest, beatings, and head cracking on picket lines and at political demonstrations. Special squads were assigned to sanitary inspections of tenements and such "nuisance" industries as slaughterhouses and fat boiling. The NYPD also oversaw the work of the Board of Elections. The job of police reporter, therefore, offered the opportunity for the most comprehensive coverage—and understanding—of city life.[9]

Riis's police reporting from these years reflected the expansive domain of the NYPD, and the bulk of his writing addressed roughly

FIGURE 1.2 "Shelter for the Homeless—Night Scene in a New York Station House," *Harper's Weekly*, December 13, 1873. Collection of the New-York Historical Society.

four general groups of subjects from the vantage of daily police work: the obscure and transient sides of New York life; mostly celebratory accounts of the work and history of the NYPD; "human interest" sketches heavily dependent upon racial and ethnic typing; and sanitation and health issues, especially in the rapidly growing tenement districts. His editors expected him to be able to cover a wide variety of events and topics, and much of his writing reflects a formulaic approach required to meet these demands. Yet as his journalism matured through the 1880s, Riis evolved a distinctive and highly clinical approach, one that fused empathic descriptions of human misery and resilience, statistical data culled from police and other government sources, and a fierce skepticism directed at popular myth and the more sensational mysteries of the city.

A large fraction of Riis's police journalism turned on explorations of the anonymity and randomness of big-city life. If the city offered unique opportunities for remaking one's identity, it was also a place where many people lost it, as illustrated by the high rates of missing persons, abandoned children, and suicide. Thus an 1883 piece on "People Who Disappear" asked of the five hundred New Yorkers reported lost each year, "Do they ever return? Or, once sucked under in the mad whirlpool of metropolitan life in which only the sum, not the individual, counts, are they nevermore cast up to the surface and to the sight of men?" In fact, Riis found, five-sixths of those sought for turned up, and "a brief glance at the 'missing' book at Police Headquarters quite disposes of the ignorant claim that there is a growing quota of the population that annually disappears and leaves no trace behind." The ranks of the missing included many men on drunks, who often returned after a ten-day term on Blackwell's Island. "Most of the self respecting citizens whom a temporary moral and financial bankruptcy cause to embrace the city's hospitality for the period of ten days travel incognito." For women, the notation " 'found performing' at this or that theatre, or preparing for it, is not the among those least frequently entered on the police record." A related article, "Secrets of the River," described how city police routinely pulled more than 150 bodies out of New York's rivers, with as many as twenty per week in the spring. "The warm weather brings up the dead from the river bottom where they have lain, frozen and whole, all winter. . . . To look at the bundles of foul, ill-smelling clothes thrown in a corner of the dead house or laid out on the pier to dry, is not inviting; to handle or touch them repulsive to the last degree." But with this work, "Many an anxious query is answered then, many a dreadful secret revealed when the 'floaters' come," and about half of the bodies are claimed.[10]

Riis pondered the city's growing number of suicides, noting that the rate had nearly doubled between 1850 and 1880, when 152 New Yorkers took their own lives. He understood this phenomenon as a social one, arguing that suicide needed to be thought of as a contagious disease, just like typhus fever or diphtheria—only the causes were laid to poverty, financial panics, and domestic unhappiness. In writing about the annual "spring boom in foundlings," when police routinely picked up the largest number of abandoned babies, Riis composed an unsentimental account. He dismissed the commonly repeated claim that many richly dressed infants turned up on the streets as a myth—"None ever do. Money can buy shelter for babies as for their parents." Police matrons charged with sending foundlings to a nursery on Randall's Island found that 70 percent were boys, with two-thirds from the city's East Side tenement districts. "Who shall judge harshly the mother who casts her child from her bosom?" Riis challenged his readers. "Who shall know what heart-strings were sundered then? Now and then one can hear them vibrate yet in the despairing wail scratched on a piece of soiled paper: 'Take care of my child, for God's sake. I cannot.' "[11]

Riis chronicled the dolorous range of police duties. The NYPD carted away more than twenty thousand dead animals from the streets each year, including twenty horses each day, many more in summer. Police headquarters received "an apparently endless procession of lunatics of all grades," including alcoholic and spiritual cranks. "A well dressed, intelligent looking woman demanded a private interview with the Superintendent. She told him that some Irish people had a machine by means of which they threw a red light on her brain clear through the brick of her house, and by pursuing her early and late drove her to distraction." Over seven thousand New Yorkers held permits to carry revolvers, and many thousands more had guns without them. "No laws or ordinances," Riis wrote, "have had power to suppress the abuse of the promiscuous carrying of deadly weapons. Whole classes of the worst element in the city's population go around with the means of murder ready to their hands." Thus, especially for the intoxicated, "Danger lurks at every step in the streets of New York, after dark, to the person who has not his full senses about him." Every day police took into custody 150 drunken men and women, forming the great bulk of the prisoners filling the station houses at night. "The process of searching drunken prisoners is not a peaceful one, and frequently requires the united efforts of half a dozen stalwart policemen."[12]

Like every police reporter of his era, eager for the inside story, Riis cultivated a close, even fawning, relationship with the NYPD brass. In Inspector Thomas Byrnes, the ambitious and publicity-conscious chief of the Detective Bureau, he found a very willing partner. Riis wrote numerous pieces profiling Byrnes's efforts to professionalize detective work by centralizing it at NYPD headquarters, routinizing information gathering, and abolishing the old reward system that had often made partners out of cops and criminals. "The source of his success," he wrote, "is his knowledge of human nature and of motives that sway criminals. It is partly the result of intuition, and partly of hard study. The Inspector directs the work of his office always in person." Riis faithfully chronicled Byrnes's work in building up the "Rogues Gallery," some 1,600 photographs of criminals, which became a major tourist attraction for strangers from all parts of the country. He regaled his readers with detailed accounts of Byrnes's "Chamber of Horrors," a neatly furnished inner room featuring the tools and weapons of various thieves and murderers convicted of crime. Here, Riis noted, was Byrnes's "confessional" where he worked the "third degree" on criminals—although Riis made no mention of the physical brutality Byrnes regularly practiced there. Riis preferred a focus upon Byrnes's executive ability, his "force of character," and his psychological astuteness, and on statistical measures of Byrnes's success, as when the inspector boasted that more than 1,400 years of "time" had been given to criminals during his first three years in office.[13]

In later years Riis would become far more critical of the NYPD, and of Byrnes when he rose to superintendent. But during the 1880s Riis contributed as much as any journalist to Byrnes's growing reputation as the greatest detective in America. But beyond the lionizing of Byrnes, Riis wrote much less about crime fighting and crime punishment than of the department's role in maintaining civil order. He shared the upper- and middle-class view that the NYPD's greatest moments came in such historic conflicts as the Dead Rabbit Riots of 1857, the Draft Riots of 1863, and the Orange Riots of 1870–71. All of these violent moments had deep roots in complicated, intense political and ethnic clashes, and Riis had no doubt that the department would continue to be defined by its ability to maintain political order, particularly in "the dawn of another century that is to test the soundness of Karl Marx's doctrines in conflict with locust clubs and official muscle."[14]

During the 1880s New York experienced the first rush of the mass immigration from eastern and southern Europe that would soon radically reshape the city's demography, politics, and cultural life. Amidst the increasingly polyglot reality of Manhattan's streets, workshops, and places of amusement, Riis looked to the "typing" of racial and national groups as one way of helping his readers—and himself—make sense of the city's dizzying diversity. On one level, of course, Riis merely shared in the conventional wisdom of educated Americans, powerfully reinforced by contemporary science, that "race" was the fundamental unit of human organization. But through his journalism, he extended that belief as a key to understanding city life and solving its problems. In 1890, looking to reassure genteel readers and invoke the power of science, he urged a carefully constructed racial hierarchy as the very foundation of *How the Other Half Lives.*

Indeed Riis believed that his ability to name and describe racial and national traits flowed directly from his work as a police reporter, and that his day-to- day experiences with so many "others" gave him a privileged, authoritative knowledge. Consider, for example, this 1883 account of the NYPD's ambulance service.

> For a study of national character a down-town police station at night furnishes unlimited opportunity. Fighting Germans "jaw" each other in a voice that drowns out all other sounds. The Irishman fights more and has less to say, but that of a kind that quite makes up for the lack of quantity. He generally makes light of the scratch and will not wait for the doctor. The Italian makes little noise when stabbed. Rarely, if ever, can he be made to say who hurt him, but contents himself with a quiet shake of the head, and an emphatic "I fix him myself." Indeed, one half of the Italian stabbing affrays are vendettas of this kind. The interference of the police is too often hopeless. The very names of the parties remain frequently unknown. . . . Chinamen form a singular contrast to the Italians, with whom they share the almost exclusive possession of many streets in the Sixth and Fourteenth precincts. Their names are always short and clear. "Ah" something or other. Negroes take things philosophically. Of all, the Hebrews are the most demonstrative. They make the most time over a slight scratch, and generally come attended by the entire family, with loud and doleful lamentations. . . . As prisoners they are argumentative but seldom violent.[15]

Riis leavened his authoritative pose with attempts at humor and an appeal to the exotic, a mixture meant to reassure his read-

ers and reinforce their sense of superiority. In one of his syndicated columns, "Gotham Doings" (for which we have fragments
published in the *Green Bay Advance*), Riis reported on a Jewish
Purim ball held in 1884 at the Metropolitan Opera House.
It included "the biggest display of diamonds of the season," he
noted, along with "the handsomest women." "There is no denying it," he added, "that the young Jewesses of society in New York
can give heavy odds to their rivals of the younger faith in point of
personal attractions. They are as far ahead of them in everything
that goes to make down right beauty, as the shop girls one meets
in our streets in the morning and evening outshine their prouder
sisters of the Avenue." But this was true only for young women.
"The oriental beauty of the fair Israelites is not of a durable quality as a rule, and there the gentile fair have their revenge, such
as it is." Writing about Chinese or Italian New Yorkers, Riis routinely used the word "queer" in headlines and descriptions and
deployed racial humor as a form of ridicule. In one sketch, "A
Silver Deposit in Mott Street," Riis "reported" on how Kwan
Wing, a restaurant worker, discovered a cache of silver coins.
According to Riis, Kwan had a dream "after eating twenty-four rice
cakes and imbibing copious amounts of san shau (rice brandy). A
fiery three-tailed dragon appeared to his astonished vision, and
showed him glittering heaps of silver under the stairs which lead
to the basement." The stir caused several of Chinatown's leading lights to organize the "Children of the Sun Consolidated
Mining Company," and, Riis concluded, "many Chinamen are

selling surplus starch in order to get capital enough to join in the enterprise."[16]

Yet by 1883 Riis's journalism also began taking a more serious turn. He continued to churn out exposés of Gotham's mysteries, laudatory articles on the NYPD, human-interest stories exploiting racial difference, and all the routine beat writing required by his *Tribune* job. But Riis found himself drawn to cover perhaps the most overwhelming, intractable, and rapidly worsening problem in 1880s New York: the deteriorating conditions of tenement house life. As he accompanied city police and Board of Health employees in their inspections of sanitary conditions, Riis's reports on the tenement districts reflected a journalist developing a keen outrage and new sense of purpose. Part of the story could be reduced to staggering statistics. By 1880 over 600,000 New Yorkers lived in 24,000 tenements, each of which housed anywhere from four to several score families [*Figure 1.3*]. Overcrowding kept getting worse, as in one Mulberry Street tenement that housed nearly two hundred people in small apartments meant for twenty families. Thousands of buildings were in terrible sanitary condition, with seriously defective plumbing, and often no ventilation or sewer connections. Above the first floor, water was unavailable in many units, contributing to the scourge of diarrhea, which every summer killed some three thousand children below the age of five. Of the more than 16,000 cases of contagious diseases reported annually to the authorities, the vast majority was found in tenement houses.

Summer heat meant greater disease and death, and Riis's descrip-

FIGURE 1.3 "Rivington Street," *Report of the Council of Hygiene and Public Health of the Citizens' Association of New York Upon the Sanitary Condition of the City* (1865).

tions added the flesh and blood of misery to the statistical bare bones. "On very hot nights," he reported, "a sort of human shower regularly falls in the tenement districts of sleepers who roll off the roofs, where they have sought refuge from the stifling atmosphere of their rooms. . . . The sultriness of those human beehives, with their sweltering, restless mass of feverish humanity; the sleep without rest; the silent suffering and the loud; the heat that scorches and withers, radiating from pavement and stone walls; the thousand stenches from the street, yard and sink; the dying babies, whose helpless wails met with no comforting response; the weary morning walks in the street, praying for a breath of fresh air for the sick child; the comfortless bed on the flags or on the fire-escape—these are sights to be

FIGURE 1.4 William A. Rogers, "A Sweltering Night in New York—Tenement House Sufferers," *Harper's Weekly*, June 30, 1883. Collection of the New-York Historical Society.

FIGURE 1.5 Sol Eytinge Jr., "Among the Tenement Houses During the Heated Term," *Harper's Weekly*, August 9, 1879.

encountered there"[17] [*Figures 1.4 and 1.5*]. Here Riis still employed imagery, common at the time, that comprehended his subject as a faceless and dehumanized mass; in later years he would learn how to boost the empathic power of his accounts by featuring the travails of individuals and families. By 1884, in the grim realities of tenement life, he had found the story line that would dominate all the work to come.

The Tenement House Evil: "Murder of the Home"

Jacob Riis began reporting regularly about tenement life in the mid-1880s. Appalled by what he saw and frustrated by the evident failure of philanthropic, legislative, or legal initiatives to improve the situation, he soon made tenement reform his personal crusade. By that time the tenement house issue had already attracted the serious attention of reformers for four decades, and Riis borrowed freely from their ideas, techniques, and styles. But his autobiography suggested that he himself had pretty much invented the struggle, and it was strangely silent on many of the contemporaries and predecessors who had influenced him. In particular, Riis went to great pains to erase the more radical forces in city politics from the story. This conscious elision contributed to the aura of Riis's heroic role in "the battle with the slum," and thereby terribly simplified that history. A closer look at the complex evolution of housing reform reveals just how critical "the tenement house evil" had become, what a wide variety of New Yorkers recognized this fact, and the unique powers of synthesis and publicity that Riis brought to fighting it.

Anyone studying the history of New York's tenements, and the various campaigns to improve them, confronts a dreary and numbingly repetitive story. The long line of sanitary inspection reports, legislative investigations, analyses by charities, and journalistic accounts stretches from the 1840s; they share a peculiar sameness not least because of the continual borrowing and recycling of imagery and language of cause and effect. The complex day-to-day negotiations and textured lives of tenement dwellers simply disappear into a riot of pathology, a kind of rhetorical resignation fueled by the sheer, unprecedented, and always growing numbers. By Riis's day tenement house reform had become a welter of overlapping reform organizations and individuals pursuing a variety of strategies and emphases: evangelical and moral uplift; raising private capital for the building of "model tenements"; creating tougher and more scientific public health legislation for an ever more crowded metropolis; and the journalistic exposure of squalid conditions. New York's worsening housing crisis revealed a depressing truth: despite the new laws and stricter health codes, the appeals to philanthropic capitalists, the improvements in architecture, the more tenant-friendly rhetoric voiced by some, conditions for the city's tenement dwellers had grown increasingly crowded, decrepit, and unhealthy in the thirty years following the Civil War. In *How the Other Half Lives* Riis found inspiration in his sanitarian predecessors, but the book's angry, caustic tone revealed his disillusionment with the essential failure of tenement house reform.

The pre–Civil War generation had made the first substantial stabs at defining and addressing the problem. In the 1840s, amid a great upsurge in both immigration and population growth, City Inspector Dr. John H. Griscom published a series of influential reports, culminating in *The Sanitary Condition of the Laboring Population of New York* (1845). In it, he anticipated several of the major themes that Jacob Riis made his own forty years later. In his introduction Griscom noted, "It is often said that 'one half of the world does not know how the other half lives.' " The work of sanitary reformers required "raising the veil which now separates the two halves, by which the misery and degradation of the one, have been concealed from the view of the other." Relying upon statistics and descriptions gathered from physicians at city dispensaries, as well as Tract Society missionaries, Griscom emphasized the clear connection between miserable housing conditions and the city's high rates of mortality and premature death. He attacked the worst excesses of the emerging tenement system, including the growing practice of subtenancy, which had transformed many of the city's older houses into multiple-family units. An owner of one or several houses would rent them to a sublandlord, who would in turn divide them into smaller apartments, and then gouge as much rent as possible from poor tenants, usually immigrants. Worst of all were the city's cellar dwellings, housing over thirty thousand people, which Griscom urged the city to abolish. Many of these were routinely flooded by

high tides, or during heavy rains when the streets drained into base-
ments, and their occupants were thus forced to sleep on planks sus-
pended above the floors.

Unlike most of his contemporaries, he expressed real sympathy
for immigrant newcomers, asserting that "we are parties to their
degradation, inasmuch as we permit the inhabitation of places,
from which it is not possible improvements in condition or habits can come." Griscom challenged conventional notions of private property rights by insisting that the state had an obligation to
intervene in the hugely profitable housing market. He called for
improved lighting and ventilation standards, tougher sanitary laws,
and a "Health Police" that could enforce them. But he thought the
ultimate remedy to the city's housing crisis lay with "the humane
and philanthropic capitalists by whom houses might be erected
with all the comfort and conveniences of separate chambers, etc.
which would yield a fair interest on their value."[18]

Griscom's work (and later Riis's) embodied the sanitarian tradition that melded evangelical pietism with a scientific spirit, what
Charles E. Rosenberg has called "the creative interpenetration of
religious and scientific values." Public health measures were crucial precisely because "physical evils are productive of moral evils of
great magnitude and number." The overcrowded tenement population had created a crisis in domesticity, a theme that Griscom introduced as a staple of sanitary reform. He assumed that the typical
New York working- or middle-class family was inherently virtuous.
"But confine that same family to one room, compel them to per-

form all their personal and domestic duties in view of each other, to sleep, dress, and undress in each other's presence, and can it be doubted that the nice moral distinctions so necessary to a life of virtue, will be gradually subdued, or overthrown, the heart be hardened against the teachings of the moralist, and the wave of lustful passions become of increased power?"[19]

In 1843 Griscom joined his friend Robert Hartley in founding the Association for the Improvement of the Condition of the Poor (AICP), which for the next half century reigned as the most influential philanthropic enterprise in the city. Hartley, a devout Presbyterian, created the AICP to rationalize alms giving and charity work in the city and he organized it around volunteers visiting the homes of poor people seeking material relief. The visitors were all men, primarily well-to-do merchants, bankers, and doctors, whose mission combined alms giving (such as tickets for free coal) to the deserving poor with moral instruction through conversation and the distribution of tracts. Above all, the volunteers looked to protect society from pauperism, and the frauds and crimes they believed accompanied it. Hartley trained visitors to study and recognize those "marks" that distinguished the deserving poor—"our mark"—from the nondeserving—"the Corporation mark"—who must be the responsibility of the city. "We are bound, of course, to elevate all we can," he noted, "but to relieve none, as a general rule, whom we cannot elevate." Providing poor relief could thus never be separated from reforming character.[20]

But that emphasis on individual regeneration could not speak to the miserable realities of bad housing. In 1855, disappointed in the failure of private builders to act more philanthropically, the AICP created a subsidiary to erect the Workmen's Home, one of New York's first "model tenements." Built on six lots in Mott and Elizabeth Streets and originally designed to house African Americans, the "Big Flat," as it became known, was the largest multiple dwelling built in New York before the 1880s, with some 350 people occupying 87 apartments. The project sought to demonstrate the feasibility of providing decent housing for the city's poor and working class, along with a fair rate of return for investors. With grossly inadequate lighting, ventilation, and water, and the added burden of its identification with black New Yorkers, the Big Flat quickly degenerated into a notorious slum. Another famous experiment in model tenements from this era, Cherry Street's huge Gotham Court [*Figure 1.6*], built in 1850, consisted of two rows of six tenements built back-to-back along two narrow alleys. Designed to house 120 families it actually contained nearly twice that number by the 1870s. By then Gotham Court had become a tourist attraction for those seeking a brief tour of the congested, filthy, disease-ridden world of the city's poor. Both these projects demonstrated that although model tenements might be quite lucrative for their builders and investors, they represented a backward step in the living conditions for the expanding poor and working-class population of Manhattan.[21]

The failure of such private investment schemes pushed antebellum sanitarians and their AICP allies to focus more on legislative

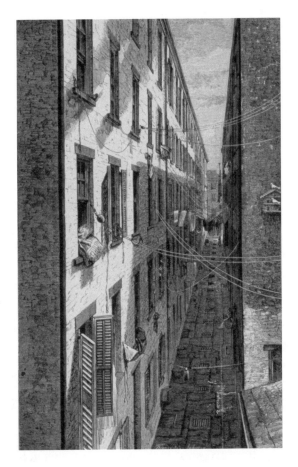

FIGURE 1.6 "View of 'Gotham Court'" (engraved from a photograph by Anthony), *Report of the Council of Hygiene and Public Health of the Citizens' Association of New York Upon the Sanitary Condition of the City* (1865).

initiatives and the power of the state for creating and enforcing housing codes and a host of related public health measures. In 1856 a special committee of the New York state assembly made the first legislative investigation of the condition of New York and Brooklyn tenement houses. Its report veered wildly between the sober, neutral tone of empirical investigation and the sensational language of popular journalism. The conclusion invoked the specter of a new, permanently degraded tenement class, presenting a mortal threat to the physical and moral health of New York:

> Here, in the tenant-house, exist the pauper and criminal population, from whose ranks are recruited the "dangerous classes" that become thieves, bullies, murderers, and law-breakers of every kind. Here, in the midst of our churches, encompassed by our civilization, is the terrible moral malaria which constantly densifies, day by day becoming more potently charged with the virus of disease. Here, around and in tenant-houses, breed the brutalized appetites, the reckless sensuality, the God-defying despair, that break out at times into appalling excesses against society and humanity. Here, in narrow courts and lanes, riots the contagion of bad example, which not only destroys those within its immediate circle, but influences to their degradation natures apparently far removed.[22]

The legislature failed to act on any of the committee's vague and modest proposals.

Six years later the "appalling excesses" of the New York City Draft Riots forced the city's elite and middle classes into a more public reckoning with tenement life. The week of bloody rioting in July 1863 constituted the largest and most violent civil rebellion in U.S. history, and for decades its memory hung like a menacing cloud over the city's political and social life. In the many efforts to analyze the causes and explain the meaning of the Draft Riots, the tenement problem, now understood as a permanent and worsening reality of city life, figured prominently. The close connections between inferior and overcrowded housing, the city's appallingly high mortality and disease rates, and the lingering threat to the political order gave more weight to scientific and medical approaches. Writing in the *American Medical Times* just days after the riots ended, Dr. Stephen Smith posited an accumulated, quasi-hereditary culture of depravity: "The elements of popular discord are gathered in those wretchedly constructed tenement houses, where poverty, disease, and crime find a fit abode. Here disease in its most loathsome form propagates itself from parent to child, more and more aggravated with each generation." Like many others, Smith identified a crisis of domesticity in the tenements—but the situation was now so desperate as to require the direct intervention of the state. "The great and patent prevention for riots like that which we have witnessed," he argued, "is radical reform of the homes of the poor. No family circle can be practically virtuous which grovels in the cellar or the garret, deprived of the sunlight and fresh air; nor can a family be very vicious which enjoys airy and spacious rooms, and is surrounded by the health giving influences of pure air, sunlight, cleanliness, and thrift. . . . But no landlord will consult the wants of his tenants until compelled to do so by the rigid enforcement of law."[23]

Smith soon became a driving force behind the first ever comprehensive sanitary inspection of New York. Published in 1865, the *Report of the Council of Hygiene and Public Health* provided an extraordinarily detailed, block-by-block overview of the material conditions in each of twenty-nine sanitary districts, performed by mostly young physicians who were employed by the public (charity-supported) dispensaries of the city. The council worked under the auspices the Citizens' Association, an organization composed of industrialists and merchants, many of whom had been active in such groups as the AICP, and all of whom had been badly frightened by the Draft Riots. The report still stands as a landmark in the history of the nation's public health movement. It emphasized the city's fearfully high death and disease rates, as these were the most reliable test of sanitary conditions [*Figure 1.7*]. Thus, in 1863 more than 25,000 New Yorkers died out of a population of some 900,000 for an overall annual mortality rate of 1:35 (one death for every thirty-five inhabitants), far higher than in English and French cities or in Boston or Philadelphia. Roughly half of all deaths were children under five. The inspection found a strong correlation between higher death rates and tenement living. In the more crowded tenement districts the death rate approached 1:20, and for children younger than five death rates of 1:5 or worse were not uncommon. For every death there were also at least twenty-five to thirty cases of sickness, from smallpox, typhus, diphtheria, cholera, and other preventable infectious diseases. For those who recovered, these bouts of illness could last for several weeks and greatly diminished vitality and life expectancy.[24]

Statistics revealed how rapidly the tenement population had mushroomed in the twenty years since John Griscom first attacked the issue. The report found roughly 500,000 New Yorkers (about 110,000 families) living in more than 15,000 tenement houses and

FIGURE 1.7
"A Perpetual Fever
Nest" (engraved
from a photograph
by Anthony), *Report
of the Council of
Hygiene and Public
Health of the Citizens'
Association of New
York Upon the
Sanitary Condition of
the City* (1865).

cellars, with an average of seven-plus families in each. With all these
people packed into two square miles, New York's most crowded districts, such as the Fourth and Sixth Wards, suffered from a greater
population density than any section of London, Liverpool, or any
other European city. Tenant house dwellers ought to be thought
of as "constituting a class, and as being allied with the causes of

sickness, pauperism, and crime." Dr. Ezra R. Pulling, sanitary inspector for the congested Fourth Ward neighborhood near the East River docks, used the term "tenant house rot" to describe the "state of physical, mental, and moral decline" allegedly peculiar to the people living in Gotham Court and other large tenements. His conflation of physical ailments and "moral degradation"—and their potential political consequences—was typical.

> We often find in persons of less than middle age who have long occupied such confined and filthy premises, a morbid condition of the system unknown elsewhere. The eye becomes bleared, the senses blunted, the limbs shrunken and tremulous, the secretions exceedingly offensive. There is a state of premature decay. In this condition of life the ties of nature seem to be unloosed. Maternal instinct and filial affection seem to participate in the general decay of soul and body.... Under such influences are reared to-day a large proportion of the future citizens of New York, who will control its social and political destinies.... The tocsin which next summons them from their dark and noisome haunts may be the prelude to a scene of universal pillage, slaughter, and destruction.[25]

Dilapidated houses constituted only part of the overall health crisis, as the inspectors detailed a range of other factors, that were worst in the tenement districts. These included filthy streets; overflowing and neglected privies; lack of running water, proper sewerage, and drainage; nuisance industries—such as slaughtering, bone boiling,

FIGURE 1.8 "A Public School, and One of the Slaughter Houses in the Fourteenth Ward," *Report of the Council of Hygiene and Public Health of the Citizens' Association of New York Upon the Sanitary Condition of the City* (1865).

and fat melting—operating right next to tenements and schools; offal dumps and manure yards near populous streets [*Figure 1.8*]. The report stressed the need for combining improved tenement house construction and inspection with the enactment of tougher sanitary laws guided by modern scientific principles rather than the influence of political patronage.

But the benefits of medical and sanitary science were by no means universally accepted in these years. The inspectors often encountered resistance to their work. Dr. E.H. Janes, whose district covered the West 20s and 30s, noted the "apparent unwillingness on the part of tenants to acknowledge the truth in regard to the actual amount of sickness occurring amongst them." Even in a house where deaths had been reported from cholera infantum, he was told repeatedly that "there neither was nor had been sickness in the house. I have not been able to account for this unwillingness to communicate information." Dr. Oscar G. Smith, working in Monroe Street on the Lower East Side, wrote in his notebook how "in several instances the Inspector had some difficulty in finding anyone, all seeming to disappear on his appearance from their own fears."

The suspicion and outright hostility the inspectors faced had a logic all its own. Visits from doctors or charity workers exposed and no doubt highlighted vast chasms of class and ethnic difference. Many poor and working-class people had learned to distrust physicians, and they feared winding up in city hospitals, which they associated more with dying than getting well. Indeed, the scientific consensus on the germ theory of infectious disease would not form until the 1880s. And an admission of sickness could also lead to eviction, a disastrous event in the city's desperately tight housing market.[26]

The Council of Hygiene's well-publicized sanitary inspection, along with a cholera scare in the summer and fall of 1865, helped propel two landmark laws through the New York State legislature. In 1866 the state created the Metropolitan Board of Health, covering the city and several adjacent counties, with nine commissioners, including the four commissioners of the Metropolitan Police Department. In theory, the new board had extremely broad powers to make laws and regulations, and to enforce them through the work of fifteen professional sanitary inspectors and the city police. The act offered the first comprehensive health legislation of its kind in the United States, and it established, in principle at least, the state's inherent right to actively protect the public health and to challenge private property rights if necessary.

The Tenement House Law of 1867 buttressed the board's authority to regulate tenement conditions and offered, for the first time, a legal definition of a tenement house as "the home or residence of more than three families living independently of another, and doing their cooking on the premises." As with the health legislation, the 1867 law established the principle of the state's power to curb the property rights of landlords and builders in the interest of the common good. But many of its provisions would soon prove extremely vague, unenforceable, and easy to circumvent. Basic standards for fire protection, ventilation, and light were quite low. A landlord, for example, was required to provide only one water closet or privy for every twenty inhabitants, and that could be located in the yard, as could the water tap. There was no limit on the percentage of the lot that could be covered by a tenement, thus encouraging the construction of even more badly ventilated, sunless buildings on the standard 25 x 100–foot city lots. Responsibility for enforcement lay with the understaffed Board of Health, which immediately found itself buffeted by the political pressures of small landlords, real estate interests, builders, and machine politicians.[27] Charles F. Chandler, president of the New York Board of Health from 1873 to 1883, complained that the well-organized lobby of tenement house owners was his most intractable political foe. "They insisted that [sanitary science] was a new and Experimental thing," he told the New York County Medical Society, "that it was a 'Board of Abstract Scientists' experimenting with their property and ruining them." Tenement owners relentlessly attacked the board's legitimacy through lawsuits and complained of being "treated as criminals" by police acting on the board's orders. "Under the present health laws and codes," one petition argued typically, "the property and interests of the citizen are far too much at the mercy of the Board of Health, whose action in most cases is prompted by the reports of subordinates, not always well informed, and very often careless, partial and unmannerly."[28]

Sanitary reformers had succeeded in pushing through legislation that provided at least the promise of improving the health and housing of New Yorkers. But the new laws were inadequate protection against powerful social and political currents swirling through Gilded Age New York: the ever increasing flow of immigrants that created a perpetual housing shortage; the continued attraction of tenement house ownership to small businessmen, including thousands of immigrant entrepreneurs; the persistent, powerful legal and political challenges to state interference with property rights. The various groups dedicated to improving the tenements—medical doctors, evangelical ministers and philanthropists, model tenement builders, professional sanitarians—were divided by different emphases and approaches, and their alliances were shaky and temporary. Yet they shared a basic assumption that tenement life led to what Jacob Riis later called "the murder of the home"—the social crisis of the tenement was at root a domestic crisis.

But they discovered that even the best-intentioned reform efforts could produce disturbing unintended consequences, as in the various efforts to create "model tenements." In 1878 the *Plumber and Sanitary Engineer*, an eclectic monthly devoted to improving water supply, drainage, heating, and lighting, announced a tenement house design competition, offering $500 for the best architectural designs that could be adapted to the standard 25 x 100–foot building lot and significantly improved light, ventilation, and safety for the typical "railroad" flat. The magazine's founder, Henry C. Meyer, had built a thriving business in plumbing and gas supplies in New York, and his motivation for founding the journal illustrated how life-threatening sanitary conditions cut across class boundaries. Diphtheria struck Meyer and his entire family in 1877, and, he recalled, "though my business was that of manufacturing supplies for plumbing, water, gas and steam work, I had never taken the trouble to examine the drainage of my own house."[29]

Meyer's contest attracted more than two hundred designs and received extensive commentary in New York newspapers; an art gallery exhibited them for the public. The first-prize entry, by James Ware, became the prototype for the "dumbbell" tenement, a five- or six-story building with four apartments on each floor surrounding a central core containing a stairway and a shared water closet. Most of a floor's rooms, as well as hallways and stairwells, depended upon a narrow airshaft for their dim light. The airshaft itself was not only inadequate for providing light and air, but also proved a dangerous duct for the spread of flames and frequently became a dumping ground for garbage. The pressure of designing a tenement that could house enough people to make it commercially attractive as an investment resulted in cramped buildings that covered 90 percent of the lot. Variations on the dumbbell design, with airshafts providing only the faintest light and ventilation, quickly became the compromise standard for new tenements. Of the roughly sixty thousand new tenements built between 1880 and 1900 in Greater New York, a large majority were of the dumbbell type. In 1903, the leading students of the city's housing problems pointed back to that design as "the type of tenement house which today is the curse of our city. . . . It is this plan which has produced a system of tenement houses unknown to an other city, which has produced the evil of the air shaft,—a product solely of New York, and one which makes our housing conditions the worst in the world."[30]

The tenement design competition stimulated other activism as well. In 1879 a series of public mass meetings, held at Cooper Union, brought together the city's leading housing and sanitary reformers, who, despite their differences, all shared a fundamentally paternalist political strategy, "to rouse the better classes to action." Press accounts noted that roughly half of those attending were women, and that the bulk of the audience was of the "better middle class," along with many more prominent New Yorkers, "and a very small representation of those in whose interest the meeting was held, sitting modestly in back seats." Presided over by

Mayor Edward Cooper, the mass meetings revealed both the shared assumptions and the ideological tensions present within even such a narrowly constituted movement.

Parke Godwin, editor of the *New York Post* and a leading proponent of model tenements, set the tone with an emotionally charged appeal for his audience to consider the crisis of domesticity in the tenements, the surest mark of their occupants' "otherness."

> Home, as you and I know it, is not understood in the tenement houses of this City. To us it is the centre of the sweetest and most generous affection; the place in which concentres all the intercourse of life, and which lifts us to a very paradise on earth. These black holes in the wall are not the homes you and I know and love. But, my friends, they are the only homes that half your people know. They are the homes where intemperance is nursed, crimes are nourished, the modesty of girlhood is crushed, and the innocent instincts of childhood are stifled in their birth. Families are crowded together in such a manner that it is impossible for morality, even in a Christian family, to flourish.

Frederick R. Coudert, a wealthy attorney who served as president of the city bar association, agreed that "it is a mockery to call that 'home.' It is no home." He described the men and women living in tenements as degraded below the level of beasts, and he challenged his audience to consider the political implications of it all. "Do you know that these children are going to rule you and your children?

Do you know that they are going to be your masters and the masters of your children? These degraded men and women are bringing up the ruling race."[31]

But some speakers insisted upon distinctions. Dr. E.L. Shafer, who had personally investigated tenements for the State Charities Aid Association, conducted an imaginary tour to show that "the decent poor man, with no means to secure rooms outside a tenement house, was compelled to live and rear his children in contact with the degraded and criminal classes of society." Sanitary engineers, such as Col. George E. Waring, tried to shift the focus to more technical and systemic solutions. Better plumbing and sewer connections would be far preferable to more charity money. "The ignorant tenement occupant," Waring claimed, "is the ward of the public. This meeting can have no higher object than to enable the proper authorities to enforce proper drainage." And Rev. Dr. Henry W. Bellows, who had led the U.S. Sanitary Commission during the Civil War, distanced himself from those who believed tenement dwellers "to be different from us in goodness, aspirations, and self-control. It is treason against humanity and treason against the providence of God to talk of 500,000 of our fellow creatures in this city as absolutely devoted to sin and misery. . . . How I wish that this hall were filled tonight with tenement house residents."[32]

The reform agitation of the late 1870s culminated in the Tenement House Act of 1879, a revision of the 1867 law that proved a hollow victory. The new law did establish a force of thirty sanitary police under the Board of Health and create a fund for the annual sanitary inspections of all city tenements. Other new provisions offered potentially crucial improvements: limiting any new tenement house from covering more than 65 percent of the standard 25 x 100–foot lot; prohibiting the building of so-called rear tenements unless they maintained adequate light and ventilation; requiring every new tenement bedroom to have a window opening directly to the street or yard. But in practice the broad discretionary authority given the Board of Health to approve alternate plans nullified these.

Thus by the 1880s, when Riis turned his full attention to the tenement issue, the situation looked gloomier than ever despite four decades of legislative reform and political agitation. When it came to the city's housing, reformers could not win for losing. But housing reformers were also guilty of social myopia. The publicity surrounding model tenements and the earnest appeals to Christian philanthropy masked an unwillingness to look closely at how New Yorkers actually pursued the business of tenements. Following the Civil War, tenement building and management in the city's working-class neighborhoods increasingly became an ethnic enterprise, with Germans and Irish, and later Jews, Italians, and Slavs, providing the entrepreneurial engine in their respective neighborhoods. Individuals and investment groups of moderate means dominated the various phases of the business—lending money, construction, purchasing, and leasing. Many of them were products of tenement life themselves. As historian Jared Day has shown, "They were the tenants who scraped together small sums to buy leases;

they were the grocers, butchers, boarding house keepers, and barbers who pooled their resources to buy or build tenements; and they were the immigrant bankers, often the most trusted business people in their communities, who took the savings of average ethnic workers and invested them in local housing."[33] The cutthroat competition within this world encouraged neglect and overcrowding, and a ruthless reliance upon the law, which heavily favored the landlord in disputes with tenants. Was the "cockroach capitalism" of tenement construction really amenable to reform?

Popular Representations of Tenement Life

At the 1879 Cooper Union mass meetings, Board of Health President Charles F. Chandler had startled the audience when he offered a capsule history of tenement house construction using magic-lantern slides, including images of dilapidated tenements. Chandler had come to believe that the most crucial work of the board was that connected to housing. In addition to overseeing the massive task of annual inspection of city tenements, Chandler established the so-called summer corps. Every August the board hired fifty physicians, assigning each to visit every house in his district. Their job included treating sick children, advising parents on health and diet matters, and looking for violations of the sanitary code. Echoing the 1845 language of public health pioneer John Griscom, Chandler warned his 1879 audiences that "One half of our population cannot shut their eyes to the miseries of the other half." In using magic-lantern slides, Chandler, trained as a chemist, turned to this popular visual medium as one way of making sure those eyes stayed open.[34]

Henry C. Meyer, publisher of the *Sanitary Engineer* and a key promoter of the model tenement movement, noted the significance of these 1879 presentations when he testified five years later in London before the Royal Commission on the Housing of the Working Classes. "Chandler took 40 or 50 of the plans which we had received," Meyer recalled, "and had them photographed, and exhibited them on a large magic lantern screen and also showed the rookeries; actual photographs were taken of the tenement houses as they were at that time and in that way we kept up the press clamour."[35] Chandler's lantern slides have not survived, and it is unclear whether Riis, as a journalist, witnessed Chandler's 1879 slide lectures—but it seems certain that he at least read accounts of these widely reported events. And Riis himself was already familiar with magic-lantern technology from his 1877 forays into advertising on Brooklyn and Long Island. Chandler's use of magic-lantern slides was only part of what might be called a visual turn that culminated in Riis's own slide lectures a decade later.

Photographs and line-drawn illustrations of tenement life amplified the sensational prose depictions of tenement life that had become staples of the "sunshine and shadow" guidebooks popular in the post–Civil War years [*Figure 1.9*]. Written mostly by journalists and evangelical ministers and for the consumption of out-of-town tourists, these books exploited growing public fascination

FIGURE 1.9
"A New York
Tenement House,"
from James D.
McCabe, *Lights
and Shadows of
New York Life*
(1872).

with the newly foreboding—and titillating—urban spaces of the city. Guidebook writers endlessly recycled and plagiarized one another's work, creating a genre based more on cut-and-paste than empirical observation; by the 1870s, one could publish a "guide-book" without ever having seen the city at all. Although sometimes citing statistics from the Board of Health and other official sources, guidebook treatments of tenement life mostly offered overheated descriptions of the moral debasement thought to inevitably accompany multiple-family dwellings in the metropolis. "The evils of the tenement house system are almost incalculable," one 1872 guidebook typically declared.

> Its inmates know no such thing as privacy. Home is but a word with them. They have habitations, but not homes. . . . There can be no such thing as shielding the young from improper outside influences. They have every opportunity to become thoroughly corrupted without leaving the house. Decency is impossible. . . . The laboring class, who should constitute the backbone and sinew of the community, are thus degraded to a level with paupers, forced to herd among them, and to adopt a mode of life which is utterly destructive of the characteristics which should distinguish them.[36]

Like Riis a generation later, the more sympathetic writers struggled to reconcile the ideal of individualism and the brute new realities of urban tenement life. In his *The Nether Side of New York* (1872), journalist Edward Crapsey recounted a grim tour of Gotham Court, made with police detective in tow, detailing everything from the foul odors emanating from the basement privy vaults to the dark, shabby, two-room apartments packed with people. "It was plain," Crapsey wrote, "there could be no cleanliness, no privacy, no chance for decency, no godliness among these hundreds of people." But in one apartment he found a Civil War

veteran who had lost his arm at the battle of Spotsylvania, support-
ing his wife and three children on a $15 monthly pension and the
rent taken in from four boarders. Nine people in two small rooms,
yet Crapsey admired the apartment's relative cleanliness, its rough
floor scoured white and its children dirt-free on their rude straw bed
ticks. That Gotham Court's tenants included people like the Civil
War amputee, a hero of the republic, was a powerful reminder that
not all tenement dwellers could be reduced to a faceless, subhu-
man mass. Whatever their failings or reasons for their poverty,
Crapsey argued, "there could not be any excuse for the barbarity
which crams one hundred families into one building . . . devoid of
every appliance for health, privacy, or decency." Anticipating one
of Riis's major themes, Crapsey saw a dismal future for New York
where a half million people now lived "the barrack life." The first
generation of tenement life had "destroyed in a great measure the
safeguards which a genuine home erects around a people, and it is
inevitable that in the second or third generation it must brutalize
its victims, and leave vice and ignorance as the foundation stones
of the municipality."[37]

By the 1870s widely circulated descriptions and images of tenement conditions had begun to play a larger role in both scientific
and popular treatments of the problem; indeed, the boundaries
between these two were often quite blurry. The 1865 Citizens'
Association report, for example, included many engravings made
after photographs and artists' drawings, along with its detailed color
maps and schematic drawings. Many of these images were routinely

FIGURE 1.10 "Interior of Mrs. M'Mahan's Apartment at No. 22 Roosevelt Street," *Frank Leslie's Illustrated Newspaper*, February 2, 1867. Collection of the New-York Historical Society.

reprinted, often with different captions, in professional journals such as the *Sanitary Engineer*, and in mass periodicals like *Frank Leslie's Sunday Magazine* [*Figure 1.10*]. They were used to humanize the overwhelming statistics, as well as to moralize about the "home life of the poor." These sentimental images aimed at middle-class audiences turned on melodramatic appeals to the security and safety of one's better lot. They reminded readers as well that in the cauldron of urban life, one's lot could change quickly. Yet early sanitary reformers expressed uneasiness with popular representations of tenement life, especially those divorced from any scientific perspective.

Testifying before a New York State legislative committee in 1865, Dr. Stephen Smith noted how "the tenant house has been described by sensation writers, with all its miseries, its diseases and its deaths. But no pen nor pencil can sketch the living reality. It is only by personal inspection that one can learn to what depths of social and physical degradation human beings can descend."[38]

At the cutting edge of new visual approaches was *Harper's Weekly*. As one of the most widely read expressions of Gilded Age middle-class culture, it framed its illustrated coverage of the tenement house issue around the work of reformers and the expectations of genteel readers. An 1879 series on "Tenement Life in New York" sandwiched its images between articles on the British army in Afghanistan, explorations of the Amazon, and the Zulu wars in South Africa. New York City tenements in this context provided just another field for missionary work in a foreign land. *Harper's* interest in the issue was intermittent and did not discuss the legislative, legal, or medical aspects of reform work. It reduced the reform effort to a Christian crusade, appealed to its readers to join it, and drew them in with carefully drawn exotic images of slum life. "It is a time worn adage," the series opened, in another anticipation of Riis, "that one half the world does not know how the other half lives, and it might almost be added, neither does it care. . . . Half a million men, women, and children are living in the tenement houses of New York today, many of them in a manner that would almost disgrace heathendom itself." Still, the implications for the "political health of the country" could not be ignored, for "there

FIGURE 1.11 Charles Graham, "Gotham Court," *Harper's Weekly*, March 29, 1879.

elections are decided. There men are virtually appointed who levy and collect taxes, and govern great cities, and decide the electoral result in great States."[39]

The accompanying pen-and-ink sketches, drawn by such well-known illustrators as William A. Rogers and Charles Graham, have a highly detailed, nearly photographic quality. By combining differ-

FIGURE 1.12 William A. Rogers, "Ragpickers' Court—Mulberry Street," *Harper's Weekly*, April 5, 1879.

FIGURE 1.13 William A. Rogers, "Sketches in Bottle Alley," *Harper's Weekly*, March 22, 1879.

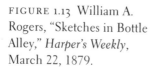

ent views of tenement interiors and their immediate surroundings, the artists achieved a kinetic, almost protocinematic effect. The specific places depicted—Gotham Court on Cherry Street, "Ragpickers' Court" and "Bottle Alley" on Mulberry Street [*Figures 1.11, 1.12, and 1.13*]—were all photographed by Riis and featured in *How the Other Half Lives*, and some of his photos owed a compositional debt to these drawings. The point is not that Riis "stole" these earlier images, but that he cannily exploited his readers' familiarity with them via journals like *Harper's Weekly*.[40]

The articles themselves may have also influenced Riis's writing technique. Unlike the official reports generated by charity workers, legislative committees, and sanitary inspectors, the popular magazine pieces made some effort to treat their subjects as individuals, with names, personalities, and colorful accents. By acknowledging distinctions among tenants and allowing them to speak for themselves (although always in dialect), *Harper's* journalists subverted the kind of lurid editorial rhetoric that referred to "these subterranean caves which a troglodyte of the earliest ages would disdain to enter." Thus a description of the dismal, cramped Bottle Alley quarters shared by five male Italian carpenters, shoemakers, and street sweepers acknowledged that they "belong to a class who save money, and when they get capital enough together, return to the old country to finish out their days." Amid the courtyard squalor, "it is curious to observe the outcropping of the feminine instinct for decoration shown by some of the little girls of the neighborhood. . . . A faded neckerchief once brightly colored, a little bow upon the neck, or a bit of dirty calico or cast off silk in lieu of ribbons in the hair, satisfies the girlish fancy for the beautiful."

A tour of Gotham Court revealed (perhaps unintentionally) something of the day-to-day struggles between tenants and landlord's agents in one old woman's desperate appeal for help from the visiting journalist. " 'Gintlemen, wud yez luk at the bit of a place they axes me foor dollars a month for? Shure it's so dark that I musht go out until the coort to thread me needle. As thrue as I live there's no lie I what I'm tellin' ye.' . . . 'You have a hard time with these tenants,' the visitor remarked [to the janitor] as he turned to leave. 'Indade I do not,' said the old man. 'They're only takin' advantage of the company, Sir. Whin I'm be mysel' I'm a bit rough wi' them, and keep them civil.' " Amid the darkness and damp, the rank odors— "worse than that of a horse-car on a warm wet morning with a full load of steaming passengers and all the ventilators closed"—there were bright spots. "In one of these we found a sunny couple, both well up in years, clean and tidy, and apparently as happy as children. He was mending a chair. She, with her white cap and smooth hair, looked on, the picture of contentment. 'We wudn't live here,' she said, 'if we cud help it; but we've been together these fifty years, jisht as ye see us now. Och, yis, it is lonesome, but we're company for each other, and that's enough for us.' "[41]

The new visual turn found expression even in the oldest, most conservative organizations and their publications. The Association for Improving the Condition of the Poor, only intermittently engaged with the tenement question in the years after the Civil

FIGURE 1.14 "The Big Flat, 98 Mott Street," from Association for Improving of the Condition of the Poor, *Annual Report*, 1884.

War, returned to its earlier commitment in the late 1870s. Its new approach included a quasi-public advocacy, as it now aggressively solicited complaints from tenants (as many as 1,500 each year) and pressed their cases before the authorities. Strict confidentiality was a critical part of this service, as the tenant "has almost invariably a well-grounded fear of his landlord—one of the most serious phases of this complex question—and dreads to complain, even to the Board of Health." Its annual report for 1884 both reflected and advanced the visual approach with a striking departure. The lengthy tenement house inspector's report for that year featured a

FIGURE 1.15 "Ragpickers' Court, Jersey Street," from Association for Improving of the Condition of the Poor, *Annual Report*, 1884.

striking set of seventeen engravings, included because, "A faithful drawing will bring a reader into close acquaintance with the regions described and will obviate the necessity of his personal exploration of these unwholesome depths."

The ink sketches reinforced a more compassionate depiction of tenement life than the AICP had previously endorsed. They showed people gossiping, women doing laundry and doing their best to keep their dismal apartments clean, kids playing games and fighting, and adults going to work. And places like the "Big Flat" at 98 Mott Street [*Figure 1.14*], housing a hundred families and twenty different nationalities, were the best place to find something called "Cosmopolitan New York." The accompanying illustration, foregrounding a Chinese man conversing with a white woman, showed a large public passageway "busy with the sound of many occupations, enlivened with the hum of many dialects, the noisy play of children; Polish Jews, Italians, Chinese and Americans, are alike intent on following their own pursuits." A Jersey Street courtyard [*Figure 1.15*], home to a colony of Italian ragpickers, "swarms with . . . females in the picturesque attires of Genoa and Piedmont"—but the picture and accompanying text focus on the hard and dirty work of sorting, stacking, and weighing. In the "Barracks" [*Figure 1.16*], the infamous tenement complex on Mott Street, the bulk of the population is described as "exceedingly filthy in their habits." But perhaps this ought not to surprise us.

> There is no water in the houses the hydrants being at the cellar floor of the separating space. . . . [Cellar privy] floors are slippery with urine and their seats foul with abominable matter, such as will not bear mention. Every breath inhaled by every dweller in these buildings receives its quota of poison from this source, and the air so contaminated is bottled up, as it were, by the abysslike cavity in which it is held. . . . Living for instance on the top floor, one has to go five flights down and five flights up for water, and the same distance in order to dispose of waste and refuse. Recruits to the army of "the great unwashed" are rapidly obtained, and the familiar pail of what belongs in the sewer, standing adjacent to the door, speaks for those

from whom no better should be expected, deprived as they are practically from the opportunity of doing better.[42]

By the early 1880s, then, sources as diverse as Board of Health President Charles Chandler, sensational guidebooks to the "secrets of the great city," popular magazines like *Frank Leslie's* and *Harper's Weekly,* and the AICP had all made photographs or engravings a key component in their treatment of tenement life. Chandler's lantern slides, while largely technical in nature, demonstrated the power of projected images to arouse the conscience of large audiences. The drawings in the popular press suggested that visual representations could create a more empathic picture of tenement life, while sometimes subverting or contradicting the accompanying prose. Jacob Riis's success in publicizing the tenement issue would owe a great deal to his new synthesis of these visual techniques, a blending of the scientific and technical with the sentimental and familiar.

Crises of the 1880s:
Riis's Awakening

Riis's full engagement with the issues of tenements and poverty flowed naturally from his work on the police beat. But two New York writers and activists helped spark a newfound sense of urgency in him, creating a hunger for more analytical approaches and a

FIGURE 1.16
"The Barracks,
Mott Street,"
from Association
for Improving of
the Condition of
the Poor, *Annual
Report*, 1884.

greater awareness of the potential power of journalistic reports. One of these influences he would forever celebrate and acknowledge; the other he never publicly recognized. Both are important for understanding the evolution of Riis's thought and writing, and the conscious erasure of one from the historical record offers insight into Riis's response to the deepening political and social tensions in 1880s New York.

In early 1884 Riis reported on a series of fiery public lectures on "The Tenement House Question" delivered by Felix Adler (1850–1931), founder and leader of the Society for Ethical Culture. Adler had grown up in New York City, son of a prominent Reform rabbi who had emigrated from Germany in the 1850s. As a boy, accompanying his mother on charitable visits, he had become familiar with the life of the city's Jewish poor. After graduating from Columbia and earning a PhD from the University of Heidelberg, he created the Ethical Culture movement in 1876 with the help of some of the city's most prominent German-Jewish businessmen and professionals. His goal was to unite the rituals and traditions of Reform Judaism with an activist, scientific, and universalist approach to the social ills of the industrial era, emphasizing "Deed, Not Creed." As historian Moses Rischin wryly observed, the Reform Jew Adler became "New York's first advocate and practitioner of social Christianity." Riis acknowledged Adler's influence on his thinking in several of his books; the autobiography, for example, awkwardly noted that "Adler, the Jew or heretic," was "among the strongest of moral forces in Christian New York." But Adler's specific contributions to the ideas later associated with Riis are striking.[43]

Adler fused a fierce moralism with articulate and specific proposals, a combination that no doubt appealed to Riis. Adler's analysis emphasized the fundamental decency and humanity of tenement dwellers, and he disputed the notion that they were by nature filthy and undeserving of better homes. In a word, he argued, "It is not the squalid people that make the squalid houses, but the squalid

houses that make the squalid people." Adler urged housing reformers to push forward on several familiar fronts—building model tenements, lobbying for tougher legislation, using the pulpit and press
to spread their message—but he brought fresh energy and new ideas
to the struggle. As a moralist, Adler attacked "the greed of capitalists
who seek out of the miseries of the poor their 10, 15, and 20 per
cent," and he charged the wealthy classes with "the most criminal
of indifference." He invoked the antislavery movement in calling
for "a great agitation, a mighty reform, a new abolition movement"
aimed at elevating the housing conditions of the laboring classes.
He acknowledged the efforts of the model tenement movement,
but the problem was that "the real model tenement house has never
been built: one that is satisfactory in the four points of air, light,
ventilation and fire escape."[44]

Adler's lecture series received a great deal of publicity in the city
press—not all of it sympathetic—and largely in response to his agitation the New York state legislature created a Tenement House
Commission, the first state-sponsored investigation in nearly thirty
years. Along with several legislators the commission included Adler
and several others active in tenement and sanitary reform. Reporting
for the *Tribune*, Riis attended all the hearings in the fall and winter
of 1884–85, listening intently to the testimony given by landlords,
agents, charity workers, architects, and sanitary inspectors (but no
tenants). Adler emerged as the driving force on the commission,
asking the most probing questions and demanding more careful
statistical data. He continued to offer public lectures in which he

established himself as the most tenant-friendly voice. He alone, for example, acknowledged the extreme tightness of the housing market, emphasizing how "Tenement occupants are in deadly fear of their landlords. The tyranny which landlords exercise over tenants is seldom appreciated."[45]

Adler combined calls for greater state intervention with appeals to more traditional philanthropic work aimed at somehow overcoming the landlord/tenant barrier. The fact that many owners never went near their tenements meant "it was an agent who stood between the pocket and the conscience." Adler praised the work of female reformers such as Octavia Hill, who had taken over management of fourteen tenements in London's grim Marleybone Parish with great success. Her hands-on approach combined personally collecting rent every week (to promote self-respect and make a profit), keeping the halls and stairs scrupulously clean (to help tenants develop good habits), providing common rooms for meetings, and taking children on excursions. Adler—and later Riis—found the gendered aspect of this plan very attractive as well, commending her example to the women of New York. Women, Adler asserted, "were better suited to work among the poor than men, and here was a new career opened for women of culture."[46]

But Hill's approach could never solve the problems of large unsanitary houses, absentee landlords, or the need for tougher sanitary standards in new tenements. Adler proposed a more radical approach: formation of a private corporation, capitalized with loans from the city or state, with a charter to rebuild bad tenements and erect new ones. Profits would be limited to 4 percent, plus 2 percent for an insurance fund to help needy tenants in hard times. Adler was thus the first housing reformer to propose using public money to improve the city's housing stock — or, in the context of the 1880s, perhaps it is more accurate to say he urged using state funds to subsidize the "business philanthropy" that was much talked about yet rarely manifested. Either way, he was some fifty years ahead of his time, as these kinds of subsidies would not be created until the New Deal era. And for the vast majority, inevitably untouched by the vague promises of model tenements, Christian charity, or any other kind, was not enough. In Adler's view, "the law of morality and common decency binds the Government to see to it that these houses shall not prove fatal to the lives and morality of the inmates. If the houses are overcrowded the Government must interfere. It must compel a reduction of the number of inmates, enforce renovation at the expense of the landlord, and where that is no longer possible, must dismantle the houses and remove them from existence."[47]

Adler thus broke with the mainstream of housing reformers by arguing that the state had to more aggressively challenge private property rights to protect tenants and public health. State action was most urgent, he argued, for razing perhaps the single worst plague spot in New York: "It is 'The Bend' in Baxter and Mulberry streets, and is one of the most abominable places that exist on the face of the earth." The two blocks contained more than fifty of the oldest, most dilapidated (but still quite profitable) rear tenements in the city; the mortality rate for children under five there was over 65 percent. Anticipating the centerpiece of Riis's own crusade a few years later, Adler called for the city to condemn the properties and pay off their owners. "It is next to useless to try to disinfect 'The Bend,' " Adler argued. "The whole of it should be torn down."[48]

The final report of the 1884 Tenement House Commission revealed that, despite some gradual improvements, the overall health and sanitary conditions for tenants were worsening. The city now had more than 26,000 tenements, nearly double the roughly 15,000 counted in the Citizens' Association report twenty years earlier. Most glaringly, a close inspection of a large sample of 968 of these (housing some 37,000 people) found that the annual death rate in tenements as a proportion of the total city death rate had increased from 51.1 per thousand in 1876 (14,900:29,152) to 56.5 in 1884 (19,801:35,044), a jump of over 10 percent. The proportion would undoubtedly be greater "were it not that so many occupants of tenement houses when taken sick go to the charity hospitals to die," where their deaths were officially registered. The trend indicated "either an increase in the proportion of tenements to other dwelling in the city, or a persistent increase in the death rate of tenements, or both." The highest death and sickness rates were found in the more than 3,000 rear tenements, where light, ventilation, and running water were scarcest.

Inadequate plumbing and water remained the biggest threat to public health. Chief Inspector Frederick Owen noted that only 30 percent of tenements provided water closets anywhere in the building; old-fashioned privy vaults and school sinks in the basement, rarely cleaned and often overflowing, were the biggest source of tenant complaints. Only a small fraction of tenements provided water above the first floor. His survey also found that "the majority of bedrooms are without light and air; and that the 'light-shaft' so called is useless." The law under which the Board of Health operated very narrowly defined an unsanitary building as one that actually contained infectious disease, ignoring the conditions that favored the spread of sickness. The overall conditions found in New York tenements, Owen concluded, contradicted "the statement frequently made, that the dirty habits of the laboring classes make it impossible to give them decent accommodations, and, therefore reform must begin with them and not their buildings."[49] The 1884 commission made numerous recommendations, a few of which eventually resulted in minor amendments to the tenement codes in 1887. These included an increase in the number of sanitary police from thirty to forty-five; requiring landlords to provide one water closet for every fifteen, as opposed to twenty, inhabitants; creation of a tenement house registry with the Board of Health; and creation of a permanent Tenement House Commission consisting of the mayor and several city commissioners.

But the gap between the energy, idealism, and publicity generated by Adler and his fellow investigators and the largely ineffectual legislation that followed greatly disappointed the reform movement. And even when significant laws were passed, the specter of legal opposition and a conservative judiciary loomed. This was the bitter lesson of the landmark 1885 court decision *In re Jacobs*, in which

FIGURE 1.17 "Tenement House Tobacco Strippers—Employment of Children in Violation of the Law," *Frank Leslie's Illustrated Newspaper*, January 28, 1888. Collection of the New-York Historical Society.

the New York State Court of Appeals declared unconstitutional a law prohibiting cigar manufacturing in tenement houses. The campaign to outlaw the cigar-making trade in tenements—where families made cigars in apartments rented from employers—had roots in the 1870s' organizing efforts of the Cigar Makers International Union led by Samuel Gompers. The union invoked health and sanitary issues, but it also viewed the home manufacture of cigars by Bohemian families as a threat to its own vision of a masculine artisanal work culture. In 1883, after Gompers gave him a personal tour of tenement cigar making, the young assemblyman Theodore

FIGURE 1.18 Jacob Riis, "Bohemian Cigar Workers" 1890, modern print from vintage negative, Jacob A. Riis Collection, MCNY, 90.13.4.150. In *How the Other Half Lives* (1890), Riis photographed and wrote about Bohemian cigar makers at work in their homes.

Roosevelt became the chief sponsor for the bill. He later recalled his disillusionment with the *Jacobs* decision, "which first waked me to a dim and partial understanding of the fact that the courts were not necessarily the best judges of what should be done to better social and industrial conditions" [*Figures 1.17 and 1.18*].

The Court of Appeals ignored actual conditions in the tenements and held that the law "arbitrarily deprives [the cigar maker] of his property and some portion of his personal liberty." Even more troubling for sanitarians, the court appeared to challenge the legislature's power to regulate public health: if such a law "destroys or takes away the property of a citizen, or interferes with his personal liberty, then it is for the courts to scrutinize the act and see whether it really relates to and is convenient and appropriate to promote the public health." The law, the court held, had nothing at all to do with public health, and therefore represented an illegitimate exercise of the police power. "Such governmental interferences," it concluded, "disturb the normal adjustments of the social fabric, and usually derange the delicate and complicated machinery of industry and cause a score of ills while attempting the removal of one."[50]

After he became famous in 1890 Riis would always acknowledge the influence on his own thinking of Felix Adler. But he never mentioned the work of another member of the 1884 Tenement House Commission, who the evidence suggests had a far greater impact on Riis's analytical thinking and writing techniques as he transformed himself from just another New York police reporter into an internationally acclaimed photographer and powerful advocate for the urban poor. The specifics of that influence, along with Riis's presumed reasons for denying it, are worth considering in detail.

Charles F. Wingate (1847–1909) was educated in the city's public schools and graduated from Cooper Union. After a brief stint in the mercantile trade, Wingate turned to professional journalism and by the mid-1870s had established himself as a newspaper reporter, magazine editor, and features writer. Among his best-known efforts was a detailed, proto-muckraking series on the Tweed Ring and municipal corruption published in the *North American Review*. In 1875 he edited *Views and Interviews on Journalism*, a collection of interviews with and addresses by the nation's leading newspaper and magazine editors. Wingate was thus one of the first writers to assess the emerging journalism profession and the impact of mass-circulation newspapers on American culture. In 1877, when Henry C. Meyer founded the *Sanitary Engineer*, he hired Wingate as his managing editor even though "at that time he had no technical knowledge of the matters to be discussed." But Meyer credited Wingate with interesting him in the tenement house problem, and the young journalist helped conceive and direct the model tenement competition. Wingate's relative John Bowne was an officer in the Association for Improving the Condition of the Poor, and he had evidently assisted him in the preparation of its annual reports. Wingate would soon be among the first Americans to be identified as a "sanitary engineer," although it is unlikely that he ever had any formal engineering training or experience. In the early 1880s he lectured and wrote regularly on the health benefits of modern plumbing, ventilation, and drainage, and not just for the tenement classes: he suggested archly the need to create an "Association for Improving the Condition of the Rich" to educate the wealthy about the unsanitary conditions in their own homes.[51]

Wingate's reinvention of himself as a sanitary engineer did not mean an abandonment of journalism. While serving on the 1884 Tenement House Commission, he published a remarkable series of nine articles on tenement life in the *New York Tribune*, Riis's paper.[52] Read today, they seem to constitute an uncanny blueprint for *How the Other Half Lives*. At the very least, they anticipated much of the stylistic approach, tone, and organizational framework deployed by Riis, as well as the internal contradictions in his analysis. The point is not that Riis "stole" the idea for his book. But at this key moment in Riis's career—energized by Adler and the work of the THC, yet terribly frustrated by the *Jacobs* decision and the snail's pace of tenement reform—Wingate pointed toward a new kind of activist journalism that Riis would fully develop on his own, and that ultimately made him the most successful publicist ever for tenement house reform. Wingate and the *Tribune* touted his firsthand, personal journalistic inspection of tenement neighborhoods (in the company of a police officer) with an emphasis on the actual material conditions to be found there. But he felt the limits of words. Even the most nuanced prose descriptions of "these hot, fetid, stuffy and grimy dens, with their stupefied and degraded inmates herded together, in search of warmth" seemed unequal to the task of communicating the awful conditions that he found. "Only the pencil of Rembrandt or the crayon of Dore could do justice to the surroundings"—only an artist making visual representations could truly convey "the culmination of squalor and picturesque dilapidation."[53]

As Riis would later do, Wingate organized his articles around two very different kinds of categories, "race" and place. His first two articles focused respectively on the burgeoning Italian and Jewish ("Hebrew") immigrant colonies in lower Manhattan, both of which were beginning an extraordinary period of growth via mass immigration. The idea of analysis by "race" (or nationality) was just then becoming apart of the "scientific" approach to poverty and other social ills. Earlier accounts of the tenement problem, such as the AICP reports, the 1865 Citizens' Association report, or articles in popular magazines, had all included generalizations about various immigrant groups and their "character." The 1884 Tenement House Commission, as part of its insistence upon the need for a more factual and statistical treatment, began incorporating "the characteristics of the different nationalities with regard to their comparative cleanliness" into its tables and charts. Thus it had concluded that "the Germans are decidedly in advance, and are followed by the French, English, Americans, Irish, Polish Jews and Italians in the order named." The "ranking" of nationalities would become an important element in *How the Other Half Lives*, serving as both a reassuring cultural "mapping" of exotic others for its genteel audience and an invocation of modern scientific thinking. Social Darwinists routinely applied evolutionary theory to their understanding of the "struggle for existence" among "races," creating typologies that would help assuage the fears of the Protestant middle class as "new immigrants" poured in from southern and eastern Europe.[54]

For Wingate and later Riis, such generalizations exposed deep tensions between the urge to rank nationalities and the desire to make distinctions among individuals and families. Wingate wrote that "Polish Hebrews are very filthy in their personal habits" and "their thrift is a source of evil, as it incites to filthy habits and herding together in hovels to save money." Yet in the same article he praised the intelligence, wit, and drive of Jewish shopkeepers, peddlers, manufacturers, and teachers, all working and living in the most difficult of conditions. Tenement houses were full of people cooking, eating, cleaning, working, gossiping, arguing politics—but his conclusion asked, "Is it not mockery to call such places 'homes'?" The middle-class Protestant ideal of home life still hovered over all else as the ultimate standard of goodness and evolutionary progress.[55]

Wingate's articles that focused on place—the city's oldest tenements in the First and Fourth Wards—were more consistently empathic. Here the focus was not ethnicity but the numbing poverty to be found in the shadows of Trinity Church, the Brooklyn Bridge, and Wall Street [*Figures 1.19 and 1.20*]. Nearly all of the houses here began as fine private dwellings, converted into tenement houses as commerce and the wealthy moved uptown. Largely untouched by sanitary improvements, "places may be found in precisely the same condition as they were twenty years ago, and the descriptions of them in early health reports and documents would serve equally well today." At the Greenwich Street public school, just behind Trinity Church, Wingate was astonished to find how many children had never had a bath, visited Central Park or Coney Island, or traveled on an elevated railroad. Nearly every one said their chief food was bread and coffee—and these were by no means the poorest. In

FIGURE 1.19
[Untitled], from
Association for
Improving of the
Condition of the
Poor, *Annual Report*,
1884.

FIGURE 1.20
[Untitled], from
Association for
Improving of the
Condition of the
Poor, *Annual
Report*, 1884.

102 Washington Street he found one mother, with five children, working at home sewing lace on undergarments, earning about 25 cents a day. "Confusion and disorder prevailed, as might have been expected, but there was no dirt. Who could keep these dingy and broken walls and floors neat with the care of such a family and having to earn a living besides?" But rather than address the issue of wages and sweated labor, Wingate instead invoked Christian charity. He noted the success of Ellen Collins, a benevolent Quaker, who had adapted the methods of Octavia Hill in taking over management of six tenements on Water and Roosevelt Streets. She had (supposedly) banished drinking and fighting from her buildings and lowered the mortality rate as well. "This is the bright side of the picture as it shows what can be done by quiet energy, persistency and faith to improve conditions in the worst sections of the city."[56]

Wingate thought "few citizens of New York have any true conception of the tenement question," due to ignorance, too many sensational and exaggerated accounts, and "a mistaken notion that the sufferings of the poor are unavoidable." And every candid observer, Wingate believed, "must admit that even in the worst tenements people thrive and are contented." Yet his exclusionary conception of the city's "citizens" conveniently dismissed, as Riis would later do, the majority of New Yorkers who lived in tenements. The public had to be convinced that "the bulk of the overcrowding, uncleanliness, sickness and mortality in tenements is not 'providential,' but is due to man's neglect, cruelty and stupidity. Before initiating improvement, it must first be shown to be possible." But Wingate, like Riis after him, could never quite reconcile the invocation of scientific method and a nonsectarian spirit with moralistic appeals to a very narrowly conceived "public." The "popular enlightenment and agitation" that Wingate called for and Riis delivered would certainly be aimed more at pricking the conscience of the city's well-to-do—their patrons and readers—than at mobilizing tenement dwellers themselves. Writing in 1885 for a Catholic magazine on "The Moral Side of the Tenement House Problem," Wingate stressed the need for private individuals and charities to make greater hands-on efforts in helping more deserving tenement families, as "one of the greatest misfortunes of the respectable poor [is] that they cannot escape contact with debased and disagreeable people." What New York needed above all, he concluded, was "a revival of civic pride in her citizens to stimulate them to give their time and thought as well as their money to public duties."[57]

Wingate admitted his effort to be "superficial and unsatisfactory." Indeed, he suggested (and one imagines Riis taking note) "a volume could be written about the interesting and varied features of metropolitan life among the Chinese, the Bohemians, in the French Quarter, and in Little Africa. But I confess the task is not a congenial one. There would of necessity be too many shadows in the picture and I fear my readers would grow weary." But his dissatisfaction may also have reflected deeper frustrations with the contradictions embedded in his own approach. For even as Wingate invoked and celebrated some of the more traditional solutions—Christian charity, model tenements, moral education—he argued that more attention must be paid to ameliorating the physical suffering, high death and disease rates, filth, and insufferable overcrowding in the tenements. Wingate the sanitarian saw a bigger picture than Wingate the moralist. He devoted an entire article to excoriating the city for its failure to develop rapid transit, the best long-term solution for lower Manhattan's chronic congestion. Strict adherence to sanitary codes, already inscribed in law but too often unenforced, was worth far more than stale proselytizing and charitable appeals. In his concluding article, Wingate linked tenement reform to need for more public parks, public baths, and public laundries; to public technical schools; to paving streets and improving sewers; and to purifying milk and food. "People are beginning to realize," he argued, "that society must protect itself by imposing checks on the greed of unscrupulous men who prey on the weak and the ignorant." In short, the latent power of the state must be harnessed: "Agitation and appeals to enlightened self interest will do much to effect improvements, but a law which is sustained by public approval and which compels landlords to correct existing defects is the best public educator."[58]

If Wingate's journalism provided a template for Riis, why did his influence remain unacknowledged? The answer may lie in Wingate's turn toward political activism, specifically his growing affiliation with the organized labor movement, from which Riis always kept his distance. Beginning in the late 1870s Wingate served as a key technical adviser to Samuel Gompers and the cigar makers union in their legislative campaign to abolish tenement cigar manufacturing. After his work on the Tenement House Commission, Wingate used his influence within the labor movement to make it part of the successful Albany lobbying to amend and strengthen the tenement house law. The gains were modest, but for the first time trade unions exerted their growing influence on behalf of housing reform.[59]

In 1886 Wingate emerged as one of the city's most prominent supporters of Henry George's tumultuous campaign for mayor. Author of *Progress and Poverty* (1879), probably the most influential American economic treatise of the nineteenth century, George attacked the trends toward monopoly, industrial combination, and economic inequality evident in American life. He argued that a few rich landowners unfairly reaped the benefits of human labor and invested capital. He proposed abolishing taxes on industry and consumer goods and replacing them with a "single tax" upon land. His theories were regularly ridiculed in the mainstream press, but through his writings and lectures George attracted a wide following among working-class and middle-class New Yorkers. His mayoral candidacy offered political expression to a confluence of movements that had gained strength in 1880s New York, including the Central Labor Union (CLU), the Knights of Labor, Irish nationalism, Catholic radicalism, and various socialists. In the spring of 1886 a series of bitter strikes by streetcar line workers, most of whom worked sixteen-hour days for 10 cents an hour, helped convince the city's organized working class of the need to engage in electoral politics. These confrontations, which brought tens of thousands of strikers and sympathizers into tense street confrontations with hun-

FIGURE 1.21 T. de Thulstrup, "The Street Railroad Strike in New York—The Police Opening the Way for a Horsecar," *Harper's Weekly*, March 13, 1886. Collection of the New-York Historical Society.

dreds of police, underlined how every branch of the state was on the side of capital [*Figures 1.21*]. The physical power of the police protected scab labor and cracked heads in the streets; the courts routinely issued injunctions against strikes and supportive boycotts; the legislature took bribes in return for streetcar franchises.[60]

The city's Central Labor Union provided the engine for the George campaign, nominating him on the United Labor Party ticket to oppose Democrat Abram S. Hewitt and Republican Theodore Roosevelt. But George attracted support from many nonunion and middle-class New Yorkers who responded to his attacks on political corruption and the steady increase in corporate power. In early October, to solidify and build on George's cross-class appeal, and to help counter the hostility of the press and Catholic church, the campaign organized a large "Citizens' Meeting" in Chickering Hall that featured George supporters from the middle and upper classes. The notables included ministers, priests, professors, and "Sanitary Engineer Charles F. Wingate," who told the crowd: "We are called cranks, and Henry George has been called the King of Cranks. Any man who has worked among machinery knows that a crank is a piece of metal that effects revolutions. [Yells and cheers.] Henry George will be the head of our revolution." Several days later, when he formally accepted the United Labor Party nomination at an overflow rally in Cooper Union, George explicitly invoked the tenement house crisis in laying out his single-tax ideas and program for social reform.

> Why should there be such abject poverty in this city? There is one great fact that stares in the face of any one who chooses to look at it. It is that the vast majority of men and women and children in New York have no legal right to live here at all. Most of us—99 per cent at least—must pay the other 1 per cent by week or month or quarter for the privilege of staying here and working like slaves. See how we are crowded here! . . . In the Sixth Ward there is a population of 149,000 to the square mile; in the Tenth Ward 276,000; in the Thirteenth 224,000. . . . Nowhere else in the civilized world are men and women and children packed together so closely. . . . In the

district known as the Mulberry Bend there is an annual death rate of 65 in the 1000, and in the tenement district the large percentage of children die before they are five years of age. Now, is there any reason for such overcrowding? Is there not plenty of land on this Manhattan Island? There are miles and miles of land all around us. Why can't we have it to build houses on? Simply because it is held by dogs in the manger, who cannot use it and won't let anybody else use it. . . . The great mass of our people pay a full one-fourth of their earnings for the privilege of the naked earth on which they stand. And all the enormous value that the growth of population adds to the land is gathered in by a few individuals.

On Election Day George polled 68,000 votes, second to Hewitt but well ahead of Roosevelt. The ULP dissolved not long after in a haze of factional fighting, but the George candidacy, with its unique coalition of labor radicals, middle-class reformers, and Irish nationalists, and its vision of independent working-class political power, badly frightened the city's establishment.[61]

It is unclear if Riis supported George. (He had become a U.S. citizen in 1885, but as a resident of Queens he would have been ineligible to vote in the pre-consolidation mayoral election.) Riis later published at least one article in George's paper, the *Standard*, satirizing the absurdity of so many city ordinances. But if he supported anyone at all, it was more likely Roosevelt, whose assembly committee investigation of the NYPD Riis had admiringly covered. Intriguingly, Riis did write a detailed and sympathetic account of the March streetcar strike for his Danish readers, describing it as "the greatest and most important strike our city has ever seen" and "an undisputed victory for the workers." But Riis also defended the police, downplaying the use of the force as a repressive agent for capital. He greatly exaggerated the power of the Knights of Labor within the complex welter of working-class political life ("an influence that no one could overestimate"). Support for the Knights—with their culture of mutuality and secret ritual, their celebration of artisans and small producers, their opposition to the wage system, and their general hostility to trade unions and even strikes—offered Riis a less threatening and comfortably nostalgic way to express his support for the downtrodden worker.

Riis's failure to ever credit Wingate, who remained active in labor and reform circles until his death in 1909, likely reflected his own recoiling from the George campaign, his own conservative drift, and his growing identification with evangelical Christianity. Wingate's drawing of a crowded East Side tenement block graced the cover of the original edition of *How the Other Half Lives*—but this would be the only acknowledgment of his activist journalism that Riis ever offered.[62]

A Vaudeville of Reform

The radicalism of the Henry George campaign and the growing power of organized labor cut against Riis's conservative grain. The depressing implications of the *Jacobs* case put a legal roadblock in front of efforts to use state power for improving health and safety in tenement sweatshops. Most disturbingly, ominous trends in the tenements demonstrated a worsening in overall health and sanitary conditions for New York tenants. In response, Riis groped toward a new, more effective strategy for publicizing and ameliorating the dangers posed by tenement house life. He created this by fusing an angry challenge to genteel Christians to the techniques of popular entertainment and the innovative use of photography. This vaudeville of reform took shape first as a popular traveling slide lecture show and then reached an even wider audience as a spin-off book, *How the Other Half Lives.*

Riis's growing identification with evangelical Christianity seemed to come first. Just a few months after the tumultuous 1886 mayoral campaign, a local Long Island newspaper ran a short account of a "Young Men's Meeting," held in the Jamaica Baptist Church. The featured speaker was "Jacob A. Riis, a police news reporter," who offered a cautionary sermon drawn from his journalistic experience. This brief report was the first reference to Riis as the subject, rather than the author, of a news story. "He told how he was thrown in daily contact with criminals of all classes, and in his interviews with them they would tell about the same story. From a very little beginning they went from bad to worse. If a young man would resist the first temptation—just stop and think—he would avert the calamity. . . . It was necessary to take a decided stand in life, and go forward under the banner of truth. Choose this day whom ye will serve."[63]

Riis had little taste for theology and he liked to refer to himself as a "practical Christian"—but church membership and regular worship grew in importance after his marriage to Elisabeth. Raised as a Lutheran, he and his wife became active in a local Methodist church, where Riis served as a deacon. By the late 1880s, having abandoned whatever sympathies he had for the labor movement and its political activism, Riis began channeling his ideas, energy, and frustrations almost exclusively toward New York's extensive, highly organized audience of evangelical ministers and churchgoers. Reporting on the American political scene for his Danish readers in the fall of 1888, Riis noted the rapid collapse of the Henry George movement; his United Labor Party polled only 9,000 votes in that year's mayoral campaign, as opposed to the 68,000 it had received two years earlier. "That was the pathetic result of a movement that, like an enormous wave swept the Union two years ago and scared the politicians half to death. Now they laugh at their fear." The Knights of Labor was now bankrupt financially and politically: "It has no influence whatsoever. Its leaders are competing about who will sell the others to the enemy." The workers' movement, he declared, "is dead, as dead as a doornail."[64]

In the same article Riis also reported on a recent evangelical conference devoted to exploring the religious needs of New York's increasingly foreign-born and non-Protestant population. The key themes revolved around the failure of Christian churches to respond effectively to the overcrowded tenements, "where thousands are battling starvation and freeze barefoot in the winter cold, while compassionate young women up on the avenues are knitting woolen socks for little heathen children on Ceylon and Madagascar." "If the last ten years' of workers' unrest haven't accomplished anything else," Riis argued, "at least they have awoken a faint uneasiness in the upper layers of society that something must be wrong down below for it to rumble so much." Many conference participants agreed with the sentiments expressed by the chairman, John Jay, who blamed the massive presence of the foreign born and their children for "much of our vice, crime, packed primaries, bribery of voters, bossism in politics, and fraudulent and farcical elections." The time had come, Jay asserted, "to put down foreign ideas of Anarchy and Jesuitism, and put to the top Christianity and Americanism." Others focused on the decline in the number of Protestant churches, particularly in the downtown neighborhoods.[65]

But Riis found himself drawn to those ministers who rejected the scapegoating of immigrants and preached the need to reach tenement dwellers through personal contact. He approvingly summarized the remarks of Rev. R.S. MacArthur, pastor of the wealthy Calvary Baptist Church, who admonished his audience: "You are sitting there with your aesthetical sympathies and feel sorry for your poor fellow men; but your churches are locked six days a week. . . . Open your hearts and invite them to feast on the best you have, if you really want to reach them. Otherwise your houses of God will stand empty forever. See that you get some warmth back into your blood. A healthy circulation is what is missing. Too many of your congregations are big, coagulated lumps of sanctimonious-

ness." Rev. Charles H. Parkhurst shocked some and energized others in the crowded Chickering Hall assembly by throwing down the
gauntlet: "I am tired of this everlasting preaching to saints. . . . You
can't reach the hearts of the masses by hiring people to go to them.
You must go yourselves. You can't hope to make the world Christian
by doing your religious services entirely by proxy." For Riis, this
insistence on "personal work" offered the most encouraging news:
"Small bands of men and women are organizing themselves to start
a systematic campaign among the eleven hundred thousand souls,
whose physical and moral salvation is limited by the five story barracks with their suffering, unruly crowds, and their more than half a
million children and growing crowd of young criminals."[66]

Riis embraced this nascent urban social gospel on several lev-
els. It no doubt resonated with his spiritual leanings and his sense
of "practical Christianity." It provided an attractive alternative to
political radicalism, and to those immigrants who came, as Rev.
MacArthur put it, "with the flag of Communism in one hand and
a dynamite bomb in the other." It offered the comforting illusion
of a long-term solution to the tenement crisis—"if our capitalists
were content with five per cent interest on their money"—via the
construction of privately financed model tenements. "Our first duty
is to make homes possible," argued the *Christian Union* in its sympathetic coverage of the conference. "And it is the men who live in
the wealthy wards and attend the aristocratic churches who must
provide these homes."[67] Finally, and most crucially, it provided a
ready-made audience for Riis's emerging reform zeal. Rather than

attack the poor and the immigrant, Riis would instead frame his writing and activism as a direct, often angry challenge thrown down to the city's evangelical Christians, their churches, and their charities.

That same year, 1888, Riis began his revolutionary foray into photography. Riis always acknowledged his primitive technique, his heavy reliance upon other picture makers, and his utilitarian approach to photography. He had no aesthetic pretensions with his camera—"I had use for it, and beyond that I never went"—and in fact took pictures for only a very brief period of time. "It was upon my midnight trips with the sanitary police," he recalled, "that the wish kept cropping up in me that there were some way of putting before the people what I saw there." Others may have grasped the possibilities for employing the photograph "made from life" to convincingly depict wretched social conditions. Conversely, Helen C. Campbell, the pioneering chronicler of urban wage-earning women and Riis's contemporary, touted the versimilitude of her (unillustrated) 1887 book *Prisoners of Poverty* by describing it as "a photograph from life." But it was Riis who, with the help of several other photographers, first used the new flash powder technology to make pictures of the slums.[68]

Photographs made into lantern slides, which could then be projected as large images, provided the key new element for Riis's illustrated lecture. On January 25, 1888, he presented "The Other Half: How It Lives and Dies in New York," featuring one hundred lantern slides, before the Society of Amateur Photographers. Over the next few weeks he widened the circle to lectures at New York City churches, and over the next two years Riis took his show on the road around the Northeast, almost exclusively before Christian audiences at churches and YMCAs. He employed a vaudeville model for his presentations: while projecting slides, he gave an improvisational talk, adapted to the particular audience at hand. He injected liberal doses of dialect jokes, anecdotes, and ethnic humor, and the evening usually included an intermission with sacred singing or organ music. In March 1888 Riis deposited a title page in the Library of Congress Copyright Office, clearly demonstrating that he thought of his slide lecture as both an entrepreneurial and a theatrical venture: "The Other Half: How It Lives and Dies in New York. With One Hundred Illustrations, Photographs from Real Life, of the Haunts of Poverty and Vice in the Great City, Jacob A. Riis as Author and Proprietor."[69]

And indeed the press reviewed these slide lectures as entertainments. "Every place of misery, vice and crime that was not too horrible to show was presented," the *New York Tribune* commented, "but Mr. Riis was so ingenious in describing the scenes and brought to his task such a vein of humor that after two hours every one wished that there was more of the exhibition, sad as much of it was." The *New York News* reported that Riis "talked of his experiences with his sitters humorously, statistically, and pathetically, so as to entertain his audience for a couple of hours, and demonstrated that a police reporter in the course of business is ahead of professional humanitarians in meeting 'man's inhumanity to man,' and that when occasion offers he can make horrors 'beyond the pale' painfully interesting." The *New York Herald* noted that when Riis was finished, "it was unanimously agreed by the large and appreciative audience that the entertainment provided for them had proved most excellent." His May 1888 lecture sponsored by the Charity Organization Society was frequently interrupted by applause as the audience "took a serious and sympathetic interest in the gloomy picture which he presented. The stereopticon views . . . gave his hearers a realistic assurance of the existence of such dens of infamy as few had ever suspected."[70]

Riis played to these explicitly Christian audiences and their philanthropic activities. "In closing," the *New Bedford Mercury* reported, "Mr. Riis placed upon the screen a picture of the Saviour. The end is not in the morgue, nor the unknown grave, but in Him." In Buffalo, Riis "gave unbounded praise to the benevolent societies that have done so much for the poor, and said that when he saw the carriage of an Astor or Vanderbilt before one of the worst tenement houses in the city it modified his opinion of the wealthy." Riis expressed some bitterness at having his lecture turned down by some churches "[because] I am a newspaper man and a police reporter at that." In response, he shrewdly sought out and received the endorsement of influential Protestant clergy. After seeing the lecture at the Broadway Tabernacle, A.T. Schauffler of the New York City Mission acted as Riis's informal agent, helping him to find new venues and evidently splitting the lecture fees. "I am glad to commend this lecture to the attention of any one who wants to awaken a new desire on the part of the Church to go out and try to save all who can in any way be reached. . . . I may add that nothing is thrown upon the canvas that could shock the taste of any in the audience." Such endorsements helped calm fears about a realism that might prove too real, which Riis cannily understood. "The beauty of looking into these places without actually being present there," he noted, "is that the excursionist is spared the vulgar sounds and odious scents and repulsive exhibitions attendant upon such personal examination."[71]

Only one surviving stenographic record of Riis's illustrated lecture remains, delivered in Washington, DC, in 1891 before a standing room–only crowd at a convention of Christian charity workers. This account includes notations for where the audience applauded and, more frequently, laughed, as well as references to some sixty projected images. A note written by Riis in his scrapbook described his improvisatory method: "As I speak without notes, from memory and to the pictures, the result is according to how I feel." Nonetheless, the surviving transcript and list of lantern slides give us a good sense of what a typical evening with Riis sounded and looked like: a highly theatrical and crowd-pleasing blend of shocking photographic images, anecdotes drawn from over a decade of police reporting, guided tour, celebrations of Christian philanthropy, and lots of dialect humor made at the expense of immigrants. Through it all ran the backbeat of Riis's variations on the Christian allegory of fall and resurrection.[72]

He began with views of the notorious Gotham Court [*Figure 1.22*], "the 'cradle' of the tenement," which allowed him to

FIGURE 1.22 Jacob Riis, Richard Hoe Lawrence, and Henry G. Piffard, "Gotham Court," 1887–88, lantern slide, Jacob A. Riis Collection, MCNY, 90.13.2.12.

invoke New York's historical declension. A century earlier, George Washington had lived right next door on Cherry Street while president. Now, according to Riis, not one native-born American could be found among the 140 families crammed into the looming double-decker tenement, where cholera and other infectious diseases would kill sometimes 20 percent of the inhabitants. In between the views of narrow alleys, tales of murder, and grim statistics came the rim-shot ethnic jokes.

> No one but an Irishman could have thought of the answer one gave me when I asked him what was the reason a policeman was always on duty there. He said, "It's on account of them two Dutch families that live in the alley. They make so much trouble." [Laughter.] A Chinaman of whom I asked the same question outside the alley took another view of it. He just took one look down the alley and then hurried on: "Lem Ilish velly bad," he said. [Laughter.]

He described another tenement block as

> the sort of a place where a city missionary found four families housekeeping in the four corners of one room, and when he asked how they got along was told they got along fairly well till one of the four families took a boarder. Then there was trouble. [Laughter.] Another poor woman who was struggling along there said to a missionary that, when she wanted a quiet place to pray, with the everlasting turmoil of that big hive, she had to put her head out of the window. [Laughter.]

Riis must have seen this comic relief as crucial to holding his audience. As the *Washington Post* observed in its enthusiastic review of Riis's peformance, "if it had not been so relieved [the lecture]

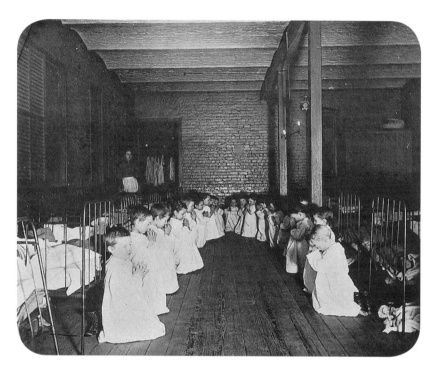

FIGURE 1.23 Jacob Riis and unknown photographer, "Prayer Time—
Five Points House of Industry," 1888, lantern slide, Jacob A. Riis
Collection, MCNY, 90.13.2.70.

would have been appalling in the sights and lives it revealed to men
and women who know little of such things."[73]

Even more than the humor, his audience enjoyed being flat-
tered. Many of the slides contrasted images of tenement squalor
with "some of the Christian work that you represent," especially
for children: prayer time in the nursery of the Five Points House
of Industry [*Figure 1.23*]; a sewing class for girls of Gotham Court;

FIGURE 1.24 Jacob Riis, "Washing Up at Newsboys Lodging House," 1890, modern print from vintage negative, Jacob A. Riis Collection, MCNY, 90.13.4.67.

the washroom of the Newsboys Lodging House [*Figure 1.24*]; Sister Irene and her charges at the Catholic Foundling Asylum. "Lots of helping hands are extended to these children, lots of them, and still there is need of more and more Christian work for the safety of the city and society." Why focus on missionary work abroad? Projecting a slide of two ragamuffins who told him they "didn't live nowhere," Riis described them as "two of the little home heathen who are

FIGURE 1.25 Unknown Photographer, "Don't Live Nowhere," n.d., lantern slide, Jacob A. Riis Collection, MCNY, 90.13.2.18.

growing up in the streets of New York every day while some of the very best people in the world are worrying about the souls and the socks of the little Hottentots in Central Africa" [*Figure 1.25*]. Before and after images were especially applauded, as in the contrasting views of Antonia Candia, a sick and abused girl from Bottle Alley, transformed into a prim, well-dressed little lady after being taken

FIGURE 1.26
Jacob Riis, "Five
Cents a Spot,"
1889, lantern
slide, Jacob A.
Riis Collection,
MCNY, 90.13.2.89.

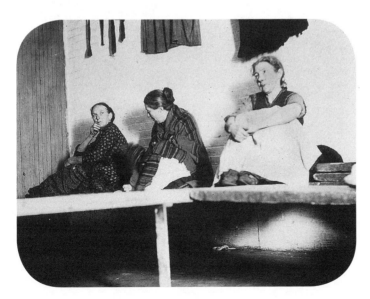

FIGURE 1.27
Jacob Riis, Richard
Hoe Lawrence, and
Henry G. Piffard,
"Women in Police
Lodging House,"
1887–88, lantern
slide, Jacob A.
Riis Collection,
MCNY, 90.13.2.20.

FIGURE 1.28 Jacob Riis, Richard Hoe Lawrence, and Henry G. Piffard, "Flat in Hell's Kitchen," 1887–88, lantern slide, Jacob A. Riis Collection, MCNY, 90.13.2.85.

in by the Society for the Prevention of Cruelty to Children. "The Christian care she had made the difference. What would have been the future of that child?"[74]

Riis's disturbing images illustrated the alternative. He deployed many of what would become his most famous photos—"All Night in a Two Cent Restaurant," "Growler Gang," "Five Cents a Spot" [*Figure 1.26*], "Tramp in Mulberry Street Yard," "Women in Police Lodging House" [*Figure 1.27*]—to hammer home a double message. One was deeply empathic, especially toward children, and stressed an environmental perspective on tenement house life: "It is the surroundings that make the difference." He followed a slide showing three murderers with a picture of a dilapidated apartment in Hell's Kitchen [*Figure 1.28*], commenting, "You do not expect a rose to grow out of a swamp, and you could hardly expect anything but such a tough to grow in such a place." But he also insisted that the poor make the right choices, and he reserved his greatest contempt for "the people who insist that the world owed them a living"—tramps, paupers, drunks, thieves. He ended his talk with a series of views of convicts on Blackwell's Island [*Figure 1.29*], its morgue, and its burial trench in Potter's Field [*Figure 1.30*], where according to Riis one of every ten New Yorkers found a final resting place. "[C]riminals don't live long. Their lives are wasted through sin. Their race is rapidly run. The last station is the Morgue where they have a rough pine box all to themselves." He ended the lecture with a picture of Jesus Christ: "Thank God! There is something beyond even Potter's Field, for out of its gloom, and misery, and desolation, there comes the voice of our Saviour, with the promise, 'Inasmuch as ye have done it unto one of the least of these my brethren, ye have done it unto me,' and also the command, 'Go out into the highways and hedges, and compel them to come in.' [Applause.]"[75]

But racial prejudice—his own and his audience's—inscribed real limits upon Riis's Christian sympathy, particularly the interracial relationships that were not uncommon in the cosmopolitan world of lower Manhattan. "This Chinaman," he warned over pictures of New York's Chinatown community [*Figure 1.31*], "you can't do anything with him. I despair of him altogether. I give it up." At best, the Chinese offered endless possibilities for ridicule, as when Riis recounted "a lesson of Chinese domestic logic."

> We heard cries and shouts and went with a policeman across the street and in the cellar we found a Chinaman beating the white girl he called his wife with a broom handle. I said, "John, what are you doing? You must not beat your wife." "She bad," he sputtered. "Well, if she is bad you must not beat her." He said, "Suppose your wife bad, you no lickee her?" I said, "Certainly not." He eyed me a while in stupid silence, poked the linen in his tub and made up his mind: "Then, I guess she lickee you," he said. [Laughter and applause.]

He could find no humor at all at what he saw as the very bottom, the black-and-tan dive: "When black and white of both sexes meet on such ground, then you have the abomination than which there is none more vile. From there the descent is very easy to the rogues gallery"[76] [*Figure 1.32*]. Finally, it is worth noting what was absent from Riis's lecture. Beyond celebrating Christian sympathy and criticizing both greedy landlords and the "vicious poor," he offered

FIGURE 1.31 Jacob Riis, Richard Hoe Lawrence, and Henry G. Piffard, "Chinatown," 1887–88, lantern slide, Jacob A. Riis Collection, MCNY, 90.13.2.210.

FIGURE 1.32 Jacob Riis, Richard Hoe Lawrence, and Henry G. Piffard, "Black and Tan Dive," 1887–88, lantern slide, Jacob A. Riis Collection, MCNY, 90.13.2.95.

no solutions to the tenement situation. He suggested no political or legal measures, nor did he provide much statistical or historical analysis. He would develop these as he transformed the illustrated lecture into illustrated articles and books—but they had no place in a vaudeville show, even a Christian one.

The Other Three-Quarters

In May 1888 Lyman Abbott, editor of the *Christian Union*, a lead-ing journal of progressive Christian social thought, wrote to Riis after seeing his lecture and invited him to write two articles for the magazine. These appeared in May 1889 as "The Tenement House Question," the first written versions of Riis's exhibition, but illus-trated only with line drawings from old charity reports. He threw down the rhetorical gauntlet that culminated in *How the Other Half Lives,* combining an appeal to Christian conscience with the vicari-ous lure of the city's underside. "Have the readers of The Christian Union the courage," Riis asked, "to follow me into the heart of one of these tenement blocks and see the sights that are seen there?" Riis brought a sharper sense of urgency to the problem than other writers, noting that the 15,000 tenements of twenty years ago had swelled to 32,000, housing 1.2 million of the city's 1.6 million peo-ple. New York's "Other Half" had long since become three-quarters of its population.

That Other Half, uneasy, suffering, threatening anarchy and revolt,
the despair of our statesmen and the joyful opportunity of the politi-
cian. Packed into enormous barracks, five layers deep, five stories
high, thousands in a block; where the water in the summer does
not rise above the second floor, but the beer flows unchecked to

the all-night picnics on the roof; where cleanliness and modesty are almost unknown, and innocence is strangled at birth. The thieves and murderers of our land are raised there.

Riis offered sympathetic vignettes describing the struggles and tribulations faced every day by tenement dwellers. He interspersed these with nods to various philanthropic efforts and rhetorical questions meant to draw readers into what he called "the battle of relief and rescue." He urged more "Christian sympathy, Christian effort," and he echoed the views expressed at the recent evangelical conference: "Get into personal contact and sympathy with those you would help. One need not live in a tenement, or next door to one, to do this." Yet even as he acknowledged that there were some decent tenements with "good and pure people living in them," Riis argued "that the best are bad; that the tendency of the tenements and of their tenants is all the time, and rapidly, downward." Tenements, finally, were irreducibly evil because "above all, they touch the family life with deadly moral contagion. This is their crime." Riis offered a highly detailed, almost clinical elaboration of the fundamental premise long articulated by elite Christian reformers: that tenants, no matter how respectable, hardworking, or God fearing, could never make true "homes" within tenements due to the lack of "domestic privacy." "There is work here to be done," Riis concluded, "and Christian sympathy, Christian effort, Christian men and women, are to do it."[77]

In December 1889 *Scribner's Magazine* published a longer article by Riis, "How the Other Half Lives: Studies Among the Tenements,"

a précis of the book to come. Profusely illustrated with line drawings made from his photographs, this piece widened Riis's audience
far beyond that of his first lectures or the articles for the *Christian
Union*. Newspapers in the United States and England reviewed the
article as if it were a book. William A. Barnard, superintendent of
the Five Points House of Industry, thanked Riis profusely for the
publicity and donations generated by the *Scribner's* piece, which
included a drawing-from-photo of prayer time at the house's nursery. Riis received $150 for the article—but more importantly the
attendant publicity and swell of invitations to lecture suggested a
way out from the grind of daily journalism.

The traveling slide lectures and magazine articles created much
publicity and a presold audience for *How the Other Half Lives*, published in the fall of 1890. An immediate critical and popular success, the book made touring even more lucrative. He kept his staff
job at the *New York Sun* until the end of 1898, but as invitations for
public speaking poured in, Riis found himself more attracted to life
on the road. One typical scrapbook entry pithily described a New
York/Ohio/Michigan tour in the summer of 1892: "Was away from
New York 10 days, delivered 6 lectures and 2 addresses, and traveled some 2300 miles and returned *tired*; got $300 for this trip." But
the book quickly found a wider and more international audience
than his lectures ever could.[78]

Modern readers are most familiar with *How the Other Half Lives*
through various reprint editions that greatly expanded both the size
and number of Riis's photographs. The most popular of these, the

1971 Dover version, offers a radically different book than the one Riis published in 1890. Against these reprints, the original book today looks small, unprepossessing, and much less visually oriented. It included fifteen photographs (poorly reproduced) and fifteen more drawings made "after" photographs. Riis divided his work into twenty-five discursive, short chapters, organized rather randomly; in the style of the urban guidebooks, they can be read in nearly any order. The enormous success of *How the Other Half Lives* owed a great deal to Riis's genius for synthesis. In place of the strict moralism that shaped the slide lectures and magazine pieces, Riis created a far more eclectic pastiche of history, statistics, journalism, and human-interest sketches, along with his radically new use of photographic illustrations.

Like so many journalists of his era, he aspired to literary art, and many reviewers believed he had achieved it. "He has written a plain, unvarnished tale," wrote one in the *New York Press*, "and yet the incidents are thrilling. The characters he has drawn and their sur-roundings have made most dramatic and pathetic pictures." Even if the photographs lacked "artistic merit," said another, the book as a whole was "full of life and color, and one is more impressed as he turns its vivid pages that the pictures therein presented are true to life, that the author is speaking of that which he knows and testifies of that which he has seen." Not everyone was looking for art. *How the Other Half Lives* can also be understood as the climax of the "sunshine and shadow" tradition, effectively combining the genre's reportorial and evangelical strains. Certainly Riis's publisher

(Charles Scribner's Sons) wanted it both ways. "Mr. Riis, in a word, though a philanthropist and philosopher, is an artist as well," said one of its advertising blurbs. But the breathless copy focused more on revelations of the secrets of the great city.

> The reader feels that he is being guided through the dirt and crime, tatters and rags, the byways and alleys of nether New York by an experienced cicerone. . . . No work yet published—certainly not the official reports of charity societies—show so vividly the complexion and countenance of the "Downtown Back Alleys," "The Bend," "Chinatown," "Jewtown," "the Cheap Lodging Houses," the haunts of the negro, the Italian, the bohemian poor, or gives such a veracious picture of the toughs, the tramps, the waifs, the drunkards, paupers, gamins, and the generally gruesome population of this centre of civilization.[79]

The litany of malevolent influences that Riis ascribed to the tenements was long and gruesome, including "epidemics that carry death to rich and poor alike," "nurseries of pauperism and crime," "a scum of forty thousand human wrecks to the island asylums and workhouses year by year," "a round half million beggars to prey upon our charities," "a standing army of ten thousand tramps with all that that implies." But he believed the tenements evil "because, above all, they touch the family life with deadly moral contagion. This is their worst crime, inseparable from the system." Even in the "respectable" tenement neighborhoods, "where live the great body of hard working Irish and German immigrants and their descendants . . . you shall come away agreeing with me that, humanly speaking, life there does not seem worth the living."[80] Riis's rhetorical claim that the tenement "system" created a permanent crisis in domesticity contradicted his conviction that distinctions must be made between both the quality of tenements and their inhabitants. This sort of unresolved tension informed the entire book and its major themes. Four of these are worth considering in more detail: Riis's deployment of history, his urban racial hierarchy, the emphasis upon Christian charity, and his proposed solutions.

The urgency suffusing *How the Other Half Lives* goes hand-in-hand with the ironic joke of the title. The book opens with Riis reminding us, "Long ago it was said 'one half of the world does not know how the other half lives.' " But in 1890, Riis tells us, "the other half" had grown into the other three-quarters, as 1.2 million of New York's 1.6 million people lived in tenements; and the 15,000 tenant houses that were the despair of the Civil War era had swelled into 37,000. The first and last pages of the book invoke the city's murderous Draft Riots, the most violent civil insurrection in the nation's history. Riis raised their haunting specter as a political shorthand defining the stakes for his genteel readers. The always tense relationship between the cosmopolitan city and the larger republic provoked more unease at the end of the century than it had in 1863. The opening historical sections of *How the Other Half Lives* represented a new, genetic approach to understanding the city. Riis traced the evolution of the tenement from the early-nineteenth-century conversion of "the decorous homes of the old Knickerbockers" into endlessly subdivided multiple-family dwellings. This was originally a downtown phenomenon, but the city's rapid growth, its more or less permanent housing shortage, and the potential for great profits made the "tenant house system" ubiquitous. "Where are the tenements of today? Say rather: where are they not?" And with "their restless, pent-up multitudes, they hold within their clutch the wealth and business of New York, hold them at their mercy in the day of mob rule and wrath."[81]

Riis blends this story with a parallel tale, the rise of sanitary consciousness, the early work of the Metropolitan Board of Health, and the allied efforts of various philanthropists. The valuable statistics gathered in the appendix reflect their newer, more scientific approach to studying and improving public health. Riis treats the sanitarians as heroic yet cannot mask his gloomy appraisal of their overall impact. Despite all their courageous efforts—the legislated sanitary codes, the Board of Health inspections and summer medical corps, the improvements in plumbing, lighting, and air standards—history appeared to be going backward. Riis's pessimism about the city's ongoing declension kept poking through, as in the conclusion where he once again turned to the Draft Riots for the apocalyptic imagery he required. "The sea of a mighty population," he warned, "held in galling fetters, heaves uneasily in the tenements. Already our city, to which have come the duties and responsibilities of metropolitan greatness before it was able to fairly measure its task, has felt the swell of its resistless flood. If it rise once more, no human power may avail to check it. The gap between the classes in which it surges, unseen, unsuspected by the thoughtless, is widening day by day. No tardy enactment of law, no political expedient, can close it. Against all other dangers our system of government may offer defence and shelter; against this not."[82]

Riis organized seven of the book's twenty-five chapters around ethnic groups, reflecting what the 1884 Tenement House Commission had called "the characteristics of the different nationalities." Although he repeated many of the ethnic jokes of the slide lectures and rehearsed some of the formulaic humor from his early police reporting, Riis also appropriated the language of Darwin and social Darwinism. He believed his readers needed help in making sense of the "mixed crowd" [*Figure 1.33*] of the cosmopolis, and like many contemporaries he draped the cultural mapping of exotic others in the metaphors of evolutionary biology. Scientific appeals helped justify a carefully constructed racial hierarchy that "ranked" nationalities against the advanced ideal of the middle-class American Protestant family. The virtual disappearance of "Americans" from the tenement districts, and the lack of a "distinctively American community" anywhere in the city, lent special weight to the task of figuring out which groups were closer to "evolutionary" assimilation.

Of course, plenty of nonscientific factors helped overdetermine Riis's racial typology, including his own background, immigrant experience, and upward mobility. At the top were the "thrifty" (and largely Protestant) Germans, many of whom had become tradesmen and skilled workers. "The best part of his life is lived at home,"

FIGURE 1.33 Jacob Riis, Richard Hoe Lawrence, and Henry G. Piffard, "Arab Boarding House," 1887–88, lantern slide, Jacob A. Riis Collection, MCNY, 90.13.2.196.

and even in the tenements "he makes himself a home independent of the surroundings." The Bohemians were "a proud race," with "the fewest criminals of all," but victimized by the tenement cigar-making trade, which they dominated. For Riis, the Bohemians represented a poorer version of the Germans. Below these groups came the Italians and the Jews, who "differing hopelessly in much, have this in common: they carry their slums with them wherever they

FIGURE 1.34 Jacob Riis, "Italian Mother," 1889, lantern slide, Jacob A. Riis Collection, MCNY, 90.13.2.90.

go, if allowed to do it." Neither group had been here long enough, Riis thought, to escape the slums. And neither was Protestant or likely to be converted either. Both the Jews ("Money is their God") and Italians ("learn slowly, if at all") come in for their share of criticism and stereotypes. But Riis also acknowledged the baggage of bigotry and grim reality of economic hardship—the anti-Semitism, the padrone system of contract labor, and the garment sweatshops[83] [*Figures 1.34 and 1.35*].

FIGURE 1.35 Jacob Riis, Richard Hoe Lawrence, and Henry G. Piffard, "Dive in the Bend," 1887–88, lantern slide, Jacob A. Riis Collection, MCNY, 90.13.2.90.145.

If the Italian and the Jew "rise only by compulsion," the "Chinaman does not rise at all; here, as at home, he simply remains stationary." Despite nods to certain attributes—cleanliness and a low crime rate—Riis held out little hope for Chinese New Yorkers. They were unresponsive to Christianity, degenerate gamblers, and opium smokers. Even worse, Chinatown made women from nearby tenements "white slaves of its dens of vice and their infernal drug," and for these "there is neither hope nor recovery;

nothing but death—moral, mental, and physical death." Unlike
the more rabid proponents of the "yellow peril" who called for total
banishment, Riis argued for amending the 1882 Exclusion Act to
allow Chinese men to bring in wives—a halfhearted invocation of
a domestic ideal as panacea. Riis saw no solution, finally, to the
utter otherness of their race, religion, and language: "in their very
exclusiveness and reserve they are a constant and terrible menace
to society"[84] [*Figure 1.36*].

Riis despaired even more over the Irish. He did not devote a separate chapter to them, but rather peppered the entire book with sarcas-
tic, even vitriolic vignettes beyond even the broadest stereotype of a
"stage Irishman." The Irish figure prominently in Riis's many asides
on gangs, fighting, chronic drinking, pauperism, begging, and the
lowest dives. As the city's oldest immigrant group, they embodied the
most deleterious, long-term effects of tenement living. They constituted a "sediment, the product of more than a generation in the city's
slums, that, as distinguished from the larger body of his class, justly
ranks at the foot of tenement dwellers, the so-called 'low Irish.' " The
whiff of anti-Catholicism accompanies Riis's treatment of the Irish in
ways that it does not in, say, his sketches of the Italians. Above all, the
Irish stood for all the evils that Riis associated with Tammany Hall
and machine politics. "The Irishman's genius," he opined, "runs to
public affairs rather than domestic life; wherever he is mustered in
force the saloon is the gorgeous centre of political activity."[85]

One emigrant to New York that Riis depicted much more sym-
pathetically was the African American, and in doing so he dis-

FIGURE 1.36 Jacob Riis, Richard Hoe Lawrence, and Henry G. Piffard, "Chinese Opium Joint," 1887–88, lantern slide, Jacob A. Riis Collection, MCNY, 90.13.2.198.

tinguished "the color line in New York" from the "racial" traits of immigrants. Negroes were, after all, American citizens and churchgoing Protestants, and Riis strongly identified with the abolitionist tradition (and later the Republican Party). He found the typical African American "loyal to the backbone, proud of being an American," and, in "the art of putting the best foot foremost, of disguising his poverty by making a little go a long way, our negro has no equal." Riis also documented the widespread discrimination black New Yorkers faced in their exclusion from trades, and he directed some of his harshest criticism of "landlord despotism" at racist rent gouging that "for its own selfish ends is propping up a waning prejudice." He thought the prospects for future advancement bright, and to those who questioned the progress made in the generation since the end of slavery, Riis insisted that people "see how much of the blame is borne by the prejudice and greed that have kept him from rising under a burden of responsibility to which he could hardly be equal." Still, Riis abhorred the notion of social equality. As with the Chinese, he reserved his severest language for race mixing, "the border-land where the white and black races meet in common debauch." He observed (and photographed) the so-called black-and-tan saloons, believing them to represent the city at its worst: "Than this commingling of the utterly depraved of both sexes, white and black, on such ground, there can be no greater abomination."[86]

Riis wrote the book with a more secular audience in mind, but throughout he held up historical and contemporary examples of Christian charity work as the most effective and successful weapon against the slum. Reports of groups like the Association for Improving the Condition of the Poor (AICP), the Newsboys Lodging House, the Children's Aid Society, and the Charity Organization Society provided a large fraction of the vignettes, statistics, and policy recommendations. *How the Other Half Lives* provided a pithy summary of a half century of New York charity work. Essentially, Riis's analysis echoed and augmented the two central premises guiding this tradition: the distinction between deserving and undeserving poor and the plight of children. Nothing made Riis angrier than the paupers, vagrants, tramps, and toughs who "profess the same doctrine, that the world owes them a living." He cited statistics showing that over the past eight years 135,000 families were registered as asking for or receiving charity—nearly a half million people, one-third of the city, forced to beg for food or other help. Ten percent of the city's dead received pauper's burials in Potter's Field.

Robert Hartley and the other founders of the AICP could scarcely have imagined city poverty of this magnitude fifty years earlier. Riis insisted that drawing a sharp line between the pauper and the "honestly poor" was as critical as ever, and he approvingly quoted their dictum that "it all comes down to character in the end." But in 1890, "it comes down to the tenement, the destroyer of individuality and character everywhere." Thus Riis maintained the old explanation that defective character led to poverty, but his entire book could be read as a plea for understanding how the tenement environment itself deformed character. Its impact was most visible on the children of the poor—"the rough young savage, familiar from the street"—too often left to the good graces of the Society for the Prevention of Cruelty to Children or the Children's Aid Society. While paying homage to their "wise charity," Riis criticized the city for leaving to private philanthropy "the entire care of its proletariat of tender years." For the many thousands of young people sent off to government-run reformatories, workhouses, and prisons, it was too late. Only tenement reform offered at least the possibility of a way out. "Nothing is now better understood," he argued, "than that the rescue of the children is the key to the problem of city poverty, as presented for our solution today; that character may be formed where to reform it would be a hopeless task."[87]

Yet when it came to solutions, Riis summarized his views in the phrase "Philanthropy and five per cent." While he also urged further legal measures to improve building codes for new tenements and to force remodeling of existing ones, he placed far more faith in the entrepreneur than in the state. The formula itself was not new. Riis probably borrowed it from an 1888 *Christian Union* editorial that argued, "If our capitalists were content with five per cent interest on their money, they could . . . provide the possibility of homes for men and women who are now housed with less regard to comfort or even decency than many a well-stabled horse." The final two chapters of the book offer glowing, if unpersuasive, accounts of successful model tenement projects built in New York, Brooklyn, and England, housing a few hundred families. Business, Riis believed, "has done more than all other agencies together to wipe out the worst tenements." The proper role for the state, by contrast, "must aim at making it unprofitable to own a bad tenement," even though reform by law is "apt to travel at a snail's pace." Riis made no case for what would later be called public housing, or public subsidies, or rent controls. "Private enterprise—conscience, to put it in the category of duties, where it belongs—must do the lion's share." He imagined a civic-minded, wealthy Christian gentleman as both the ultimate redeemer of the tenement poor and the ideal reader for his book.[88]

The book, of course, reached an audience far beyond that ideal reader. Most of the largely admiring reviews noted its something-for-everyone appeal, "with statistics for those who care for that sort of thing, with suggestions for the charitable worker, and with stories and anecdotes and photographic reproductions and free hand sketches for those who are merely curious, and who wish only to be entertained." They touted its use value for the professional classes. "*How the Other Half Lives*," wrote one typical critic, "is a volume that the political economist, the philanthropist, the preacher, the novelist and the journalist will find invaluable, because of the great mass of facts it contains about the poor, because of its information about the different parts of the city inhabited by various nationalities and because of its vivid pictures of the lives of toilers." The book could not help but educate even those readers looking for something else. "To the reader who seeks only amusement," the *New York Tribune* asserted, "the volume will furnish all that is required; but he must be something worse than a cynic who can lay it down without falling into serious reflection upon the grave questions it raises."[89]

The contradictions inherent in Riis's work—its simultaneously reactionary and forward-looking stances, its derivative and synthetic qualities, its mixture of urban entertainment and social inquiry—are certainly more evident today. Less an analysis than a passionate plea, Riis may in fact have written what Lewis F. Fried has called "the last great nineteenth century sermon."[90] The publicist for tenement reform and chronicler of poor New Yorkers did not even like cities very much; visions of the lost rural community of his native Ribe kept poking through his writing like a recurring dream. In a 1904 letter to his son John, Riis summarized his achievements modestly: "I had no special genius, no special ability. I had endurance, and I reached at last the heart of men; that is all I can claim."[91] None of this ought to detract from his breakthroughs. Riis was the first muckraker and the first American social documentary photographer. Art historians will continue debating the quality, intentionality, and meaning of his pictures. But a century later they remain a powerful and unique record of the lived material conditions in turn-of-the-century New York. Almost in spite of itself, Riis's empathic synthesis of visual imagery, statistics, journalism, anecdote, vignette, and history pointed the way toward a more compassionate and clear-eyed comprehension of New York life. The deeply antiurban impulses that had represented New Yorkers as teeming hordes and swarming masses, living hopelessly depraved and vicious lives, huddled in dens and hives like vermin or insects, now had to reckon with an alternative and decidedly more humane portrait.

Riis conceived of them primarily as victims deserving pity and charity, as historical objects rather than the subjects of their own lives. For all his talk of arousing the public conscience, his public turned out to be quite narrow, excluding the very people he wrote about. He ascribed little or no role at all to tenement dwellers themselves in his reform crusade. Invoking the power of Christian charity no doubt appealed to the vanity and reinforced the worldview of his genteel patrons. Like them, he admired the honest laborer as long as he or she remained unorganized and politically mute. In his heart, Riis probably agreed with one of the few negative reviewers of his book, the conservative editor E.L. Godkin, whose critique focused on the conundrum of urban politics. "Given a mass of human beings leading lives of which it is desired to raise the standard," Godkin asked rhetorically, "how shall this be done when the government of society is in the hands of these people? . . . How shall the tenement house be reformed by the dwellers in tenement houses?"[92] Riis had no answer, but he managed to inspire other activists and reformers to reject Godkin's sneering and set them on a path of treating cities as more than problems to be solved and their poor people as fully human. A century later, the nation still has quite a ways to go down that road.

2

Jacob A. Riis,
Photographer
"After a Fashion"

. . . .

Bonnie Yochelson

Jacob Riis is widely viewed as one of the masters of the photographic medium—a revolutionary artist whose name is known to anyone who has read an introductory survey. It is therefore especially ironic that Riis did not consider himself an accomplished photographer. In his 1901 autobiography, *The Making of an American*, he bluntly stated, "I am downright sorry to confess here that I am no good at all as a photographer, for I would like to be." Indeed, Riis was less than candid when he claimed that he would "like to be" a photographer. In the same breath, he declared a firm resistance to mastering darkroom technique—"I do not want it explained to me in terms of HO_2 [*sic*] or such like formulas, learned, but hopelessly unsatisfying"—and announced that he was "disqualified from being a photographer" because he was "clumsy and impatient of details."[1]

There is a historiographic explanation for this irony. Since its invention in 1839, photography has been a poor stepchild to painting. Beginning in the 1890s, small, well-organized groups of photographers in Europe and America began a concerted campaign to assert the legitimacy of photography as a full-fledged fine art. One weapon in this campaign, which continued throughout much of the twentieth century, was the establishment of an artistic tradition: art photographers sought models in the medium's short history to justify their own aesthetic claims. Peter Henry Emerson's praise for Julia Margaret Cameron, Alfred Stieglitz's for David Octavius Hill, Berenice Abbott's for Eugene Atget, Walker Evans's for Mathew Brady, Ansel Adams's for Timothy O'Sullivan—all of these "recoveries" were efforts to find inspiration from practitioners of the past. In each instance, the older photographers' intentions were reinterpreted to fit the aesthetic needs of their disciples.

It was against this backdrop that the photographer Alexander Alland Sr. discovered Riis's 1890 book *How the Other Half Lives* in a secondhand bookstore in 1942. Alland, who specialized in documenting New York City's ethnic communities, was struck by Riis's photographs, some of which were reproduced as small, crude, but powerful halftones. He set out to find the originals and eventually contacted Riis's youngest son, Roger William Riis, a publicist living in New York, whom he persuaded to search the attic of what had been the Riis family's Long Island home. Roger William delivered to Alland a box containing 415 glass negatives, 326 glass lantern slides, and 192 paper prints, which now constitute the Jacob A. Riis Collection at the Museum of the City of New York.

The box from the attic was a treasure trove for Alland, who

selected fifty of Riis's negatives and made beautiful mounted prints for a 1947 exhibition at the museum. The following year, Alland's prints were featured in *U.S. Camera*, the leading photography magazine of the day, and in 1949 Riis was described as "a photographer of some importance" in Beaumont Newhall's *History of Photography*, which was to become the standard American text. Newhall placed Riis at the start of a documentary tradition that continued through Lewis Hine in the Progressive Era to the Farm Security Administration photographers of the New Deal, establishing a lineage that has become conventional wisdom.[2] Alland subsequently devoted many years to a Riis biography, which appeared in 1973 under the title *Jacob A. Riis: Photographer and Citizen*. With a laudatory preface by Ansel Adams, the book was published by Aperture, the leading producer of fine art photography monographs; it reproduced eighty-two of Alland's stunning Riis prints as full-page illustrations.[3]

With the publication of Alland's prints, Riis's reputation as a photographer mutated still further. In his 1973 landmark book *Looking at Photographs*, John Szarkowski, then the director of the Department of Photographs at the Museum of Modern Art, portrayed Riis as a modern photographer who challenged the artistic conventions of his time. Szarkowski likened Riis to the 1960s street photographers, whom he so admired, writing that Riis "knew the habits and habitat of photographer's luck, and . . . did his best to make himself available to its gifts." Acknowledging that Riis "was a photographer rather briefly and apparently rather casually," Szarkowski nonetheless concluded that "Riis was intuitively interested in problems of form without identifying these as artistic problems."[4]

In the years since Alland created Riis's photographs and Szarkowski aestheticized them, Riis's claim that he was "no good at all as a photographer" has been ignored or rejected.[5] Riis, however, was not prone to false modesty. He was a professional writer, an inspired storyteller, and an impassioned propagandist. For twenty-three years, he worked as a police reporter for New York newspapers; he published dozens of magazine articles and fifteen books; and he delivered hundreds of lectures, traveling across the United States from 1888 until his death in 1914. Riis saved all his papers, annotating them for future readers and depositing them in public collections—the bulk to the Library of Congress and the remainder to the New York Public Library. In stark contrast, he neglected his photographs, which carried no meaning for him except as part of his published works and illustrated lectures. He never expected anyone to care about the box of photographs that Roger William found in the attic thirty years after his death. As his grandson J. Riis Owre observed, "I don't remember my mother or my aunts and uncles talking of their father as a photographer. . . . In his letters—I have read most of them—he never mentions a camera."[6]

"Pictures by Proxy"

In *The Making of an American*, Riis named several chapters for his shifting vocations—"I Go Into Business," "I Become an Editor," and "I Become an Author"—but did not devote a chapter to becoming a photographer. Instead, in a chapter about tearing down Mulberry Bend, a notorious New York slum, he wrote: "Before I tackle the Bend, perhaps I had better explain how I came to take up photographing as a—no, not exactly as a pastime. It was never that with me. I had use for it, and beyond that I never went."

Riis had been a police reporter for the *New York Tribune* for ten years when he discovered his revolutionary use for photography. The police reporter, Riis explained, "is the one who gathers and handles all the news that means trouble to some one: the murders, fires, suicides, robberies, and all that sort, before it gets into court."[7] The reporters' office at 303 Mulberry Street, across the street from police headquarters, was in the middle of a slum, and Riis, working at night, became intimate with the worst doings of New York's poor. Leaving work between two and four in the morning, he walked through Five Points and Mulberry Bend in the Sixth Ward, past the cheap entertainment halls and lodging houses of the Bowery, through the city's oldest tenements in the Fourth Ward, to the Fulton Street ferry, where he crossed the East River to his Brooklyn home.

Riis's search for answers to the housing problems of the poor began in earnest when the *Tribune* transferred him from night to day work. He explained:

> A new life began for me, with greatly enlarged opportunities. I had been absorbing impressions up till then. I met men now in whose companionship [my impressions] began to crystallize, to form into definite convictions; men of learning, of sympathy, and of power. My eggs hatched.

Riis had been criticized for his "altogether editorial and presuming"[8] writing style, but as he focused on the human costs of poor housing his editorializing only increased. So did his frustration: "I wrote, but it seemed to make no impression."

In October 1887, Riis read a four-line notice in the newspaper about the German invention of a magnesium flash powder, which could provide enough light to capture a photographic image in the dark. This "instantaneous flashlight" suggested a way for Riis to "[put] before the people what [he] saw" on his late-night trips. Riis, however, had no intention of operating a camera himself and "began taking pictures by proxy." His friend Dr. John T. Nagle, a member of the Society of Amateur Photographers of New York, enlisted two fellow society members, Dr. Henry Granger Piffard and Richard Hoe Lawrence, to follow Riis into the city's "darkest corners."[9] Together with a "a policeman or two," the four men set out on several outings; the photographers' interest was "centered in the camera and the flashlight," and Riis was "bent on letting in the light where it was so much needed." Riis called the group a "raiding party," which, armed with magnesium flash powder loaded into cartridges in a revolver, "carried terror wherever it went." A newspaper article published in February 1888 described the scene:

> Somnolent policemen on the street, denizens of the dives in their dens, tramps and bummers in their so-called lodgings, and all the wild and wonderful variety of the New York night life have in their turn marveled at and been frightened by the phenomenon. What they saw was three or four figures in the gloom, a ghostly tripod, some weird and uncanny movements, the blinding flash, and then they heard the patter of retreating footsteps, and the mysterious visitors were gone before they could collect their scattered thoughts and try to find out what it was all about.[10]

As Riis later recalled: "We took some good pictures, but very soon the slum and the awkward hours palled upon the amateurs. I found myself alone just when I needed help most." Still unwilling to take up the camera himself, Riis hired a professional photographer but soon fired the man whom he caught trying to sell his photographs. He went to court to reclaim the negatives and, after unsuccessfully hiring another photographer, decided in January 1888 to purchase his own camera. Riis's first photographic foray was bumbling. Crossing the East River to Potter's Field on Hart's Island, he doubled the exposure time of his first negative "to make sure [he] got the picture" and then put the overexposed negative back

FIGURE 2.1 Jacob Riis, "Potter's Field," 1888, modern print from vintage negative, Jacob A. Riis Collection, MCNY, 90.13.4.87. This is Riis's first photograph. The image's illegibility is due to overexposure of the negative and subsequent damage to it.

among the rest, not knowing which was which. To harvest his first photograph—an overly dark image of gravediggers lowering pine boxes into an open trench—he had to develop the entire box of a dozen negatives [*Figure 2.1*]. He became, in his words, "a photographer, after a fashion."

That same month, on January 25, 1888, Riis gave his first illustrated lecture, "The Other Half, How It Lives and Dies in New York," at the West 36th Street quarters of the Society of Amateur Photographers of New York. Organized in 1884, the society claimed to be "the largest, most influential, and best known amateur society in the United States."[11] With ninety-five active members, it may have deserved the description, for in the 1880s amateur photography was still a cumbersome, expensive hobby that attracted primarily wealthy gentlemen with scientific interests.[12] The society met twice a month, once to discuss technical matters and once for lantern slide exhibitions, when members shared their latest work. Lantern slides were positive images printed on glass rather than paper and were viewed through a magic lantern, or stereopticon, which projected images on a screen. As head of the lantern slide committee, Lawrence scheduled Riis's lecture to exhibit the "raiding party's" flashlight photographs, but Riis seized the opportunity to proselytize. He showed one hundred slides, spoke for two hours before a large audience, and garnered substantial press.[13] Noting his talent for vivid description and moral suasion, one reviewer compared Riis to naturalist novelist Émile Zola and to reformer Henry Mayhew, author of *London Labour and the London Poor* (1865).[14]

Approximately half of Riis's one hundred slides were mentioned in the press reviews of the lecture; especially useful is the *Photographic Times* notice, which reported thirty-one subjects, roughly in the order they were shown, and mentioned those represented with several images.[15] Riis led his audience from the infamous Gotham Court on Cherry Street, a "model" tenement where it was said a thousand people lived; to Bandit's Roost, a narrow, filthy alley in Mulberry Bend; to Corlears Hook on the East River, where the Short Tail Gang sat under the docks drinking beer. Among the indoor scenes were a "black-and-tan dive" on Wooster Street, where "the white and black races meet in common debauch";[16] Happy Jack's Palace, a seven-cent lodging house on Pell Street; and an opium den on Pell between Mott Street and Chatham Square. Riis also recounted missed opportunities, like the Italian ragpickers at work in a South Fifth Avenue alley who "were suddenly dispersed by one word from the Italian proprietor before their pictures could be caught." His tour of the slums complete, Riis showed slides of charitable organizations, such as the Five Points House of Industry and the Children's Aid Society, as well as scenes from a police station, the Tombs, and the penitentiary on Blackwell's Island. He concluded with images of "how the other half dies in New York," presenting Bellevue Hospital, the city morgue, and Potter's Field on Hart's Island. Although most of the images were taken by the raiding party, Riis included copies of photographs belonging to others: portraits from the police department's Rogues' Gallery; before-and-after photographs of a child admitted to the Gerry Society for the

FIGURE 2.2 Jacob Riis, Richard Hoe Lawrence, and Henry G. Piffard, "Gotham Court," 1887–88, modern print from vintage negative, Jacob A. Riis Collection, MCNY, 90.13.4.18. This is one of fourteen whole stereographic negatives in the Riis Collection.

Prevention of Cruelty to Children; and "The Inspector's Model," a parody of a criminal suspect resisting being photographed, which appeared in Police Superintendent Thomas Byrnes's popular 1884 book *Professional Criminals of America*.

Among the works in the Riis Collection at the Museum of the City of New York are thirty-four stereoscopic negatives that correlate closely with images from Riis's first lecture. A stereoscopic

FIGURE 2.3 Jacob Riis, Richard Hoe Lawrence, and Henry G. Piffard, "Bandit's Roost," 1887–88, modern prints from vintage negatives, Jacob A. Riis Collection, MCNY, 90.13.4.104 and .105. This is one of twenty stereographic negatives that have been cut in half.

camera has two lenses mounted next to each other, and its negative, which measures 5 x 8 inches, shows two 5 x 4–inch images, side by side, exposed simultaneously. These double-image negatives are usually used to make stereographs—pairs of prints mounted on cardboard that appear three-dimensional when viewed through an optical device called a stereoscope. Produced by the millions in the nineteenth century, stereographs, often of tourist sites, were a popular form of parlor entertainment. Most stereographs were made by

FIGURE 2.4 "The Inspector's Model," 1887–88, modern print from vintage negative, Jacob A. Riis Collection, MCNY, 90.13.4.7. It was probably Lawrence who made copy negatives for Riis of several photographs, including this illustration from Thomas Byrnes's 1884 bestseller, *Professional Criminals of America*. He used a stereographic negative with one lens to expose a single image.

commercial photographers, but serious amateurs favored the stereo-scopic camera as well.[17]

Of the thirty-four stereo-negatives in the Riis Collection, fourteen are intact and twenty have been cut in half in order more easily to make lantern slides. Among the whole negatives is "Gotham Court" [*Figure 2.2*], and among the halved is "Bandit's Roost" [*Figure 2.3*]. Because the 5 x 4–inch halved negatives are scattered among

4 x 5–inch negatives from single-lens cameras, it is difficult to recognize them as stereo-negatives.

In addition to the stereo-negatives, there are two other groups
of negatives from the January 1888 lecture in the Riis Collection.
One group consists of seven 5 x 8–inch negatives, including several
Rogues' Gallery portraits and "The Inspector's Model" from Byrnes's
book [*Figure 2.4*]. To make these copy negatives, the stereo-camera
was used as a single-lens camera by covering one of its lenses. The
second group consists of a few single-lens, 4 x 5–inch negatives,
including two images of black-and-tan dives and one of an opium
den. Riis's party may have carried more than one camera on its outings, or taken a stereoscopic camera on some outings and a standard
camera on others.

Most likely, Lawrence exposed the vast majority of the negatives
that Riis used in his first lecture.[18] When he met Riis, Lawrence
was twenty-nine years old, European educated, unmarried, and a
member of his father's Wall Street brokerage firm. His interest in
photography seems to have lasted only three years, from 1886 to
1889, during which time he was active in the Society of Amateur
Photographers, serving as treasurer and chairing its lantern slide
committee. Like many amateurs of his day, Lawrence photographed
family outings and local points of interest, such as Central Park, City
Hall, and the recently installed Statue of Liberty. He experimented
with the new handheld camera, concentrating on stop-action subjects, such as a Coney Island beach trip, a tennis match, and sport
shooting, as well as newsworthy events, such as the great New York

blizzard of 1888 and the parades of the 1889 Washington Inaugural Centennial. In later years, Lawrence married, retired early, moved to a large Westchester County estate, and became a leading collector of rare books, coins, medals, and prints.

None of Lawrence's original photographs survive, but in 1950 his widow lent some albums and lantern slides to the New-York Historical Society, which made 202 copy negatives and reference prints from them.[19] Among the reference prints are thirty-seven slum scenes made from lantern slides, of which twenty-five correspond to images in the Riis Collection. The Lawrence Collection includes familiar images such as "Bandit's Roost" and "Gotham Court," as well as several images mentioned in press notices but missing from the Riis Collection, such as of the morgue, the Tombs, and a policeman bringing a foundling to a police station. Also included are variants of well-known images, which provide new views of Happy Jack's Palace, the Chinese opium joint, and the Thompson Street black-and-tan dive. Riis himself appears in two photographs—in a police station and in his Mulberry Street office [*Figure 2.5*].

As for Piffard, his primary interest in Riis's outings, it seems, was the magnesium flash technique. At forty-five, he was the oldest member of the group and had the strongest scientific credentials. A professor of dermatology at New York University and a founding member of the American Dermatological Association, Piffard patented several inventions, including an early X-ray device for treating skin diseases. At the society's technical meeting on October 11, 1888, which directly followed Riis's lecture, Piffard demonstrated

FIGURE 2.5 Richard Hoe Lawrence and Henry G. Piffard, "301 Mulberry Street," 1887–88, modern print from (lost) lantern slide, Collection of the New-York Historical Society. Riis is shown sitting in the far left corner of the newspaper office.

the flash technique and suggested ways to improve it. He appears to have exposed only a few of the negatives used in Riis's lecture. A note on five of the Historical Society's reference prints reads, "flash light negative by Piffard, slide by Lawrence," and a similar note appears on two slides and one print in the Riis Collection. The most intriguing of these images depicts three women in a Washington

FIGURE 2.6 Jacob Riis, Richard Hoe Lawrence, and Henry G. Piffard, "Street Arabs in Night Quarters," 1887–88, modern print from vintage negative, Jacob A. Riis Collection, MCNY, 90.13.4.16.

Street boardinghouse. There is another image of the women taken at the same moment from a different vantage point, suggesting that Piffard and Lawrence, at least in this instance, worked simultaneously, each with his own camera.

The photographs shown at the first lecture reveal a variety of compositional strategies. Images such as "Street Arabs in Night Quarters"

FIGURE 2.7 Jacob Riis, Richard Hoe Lawrence, and Henry G. Piffard, "Chinese Opium Joint," 1887–88, lantern slide, Jacob A. Riis Collection, MCNY, 90.13.2.198. Because the negative for this image is lost, this reproduction was made from a lantern slide.

[*Figure 2.6*], which depicts four boys "sleeping" on the steps of a Mulberry Street building, and "Growler Ganymede," which shows a child toting a bucket of beer, were staged for the camera in daylight. Riis's literary titles corroborate the self-conscious contrivance of these pictures. Other outdoor images such as "Gotham Court," "Bandit's Roost," "Mullen's Alley," and "Baxter Alley" are less controlled; each is framed by an alley's narrow corridors and required

A Pictorial Survey of Jacob Riis's Photographic Practice

Bonnie Yochelson

Unless otherwise noted, all photographs were taken by Jacob Riis, who exposed the negatives but did not work in the darkroom. Riis's known photographs—negatives, lantern slides, and vintage prints—comprise the Jacob A. Riis Collection at the Museum of the City of New York. The images here derive from contact prints produced in 1995 by Chicago Albumen Works from the original negatives. The accession numbers refer to these modern prints.

Bandit's Roost, 1887 (90.13.4.104 and 105). Bandit's Roost was the nickname for an alley next to 59 Mulberry Street in the heart of Mulberry Bend, a notorious slum not far from Riis's newspaper office at 301 Mulberry Street. Although "Bandit's Roost" is his most famous photograph, Riis did not make the exposure. It is one of a large group of photographs he showed at his first slide lecture delivered at the Society of Amateur Photographers of New York on January 25, 1888. The lecture was arranged by Richard Hoe Lawrence and Henry G. Piffard, two amateurs who took the photographs under Riis's direction. Like several negatives by Lawrence and Piffard, this one was made with a stereoscopic camera, which had two lenses and produced a pair of images on one double-width negative.

Lodgers in a Crowded Bayard Street Tenement—"Five Cents a Spot," 1889 (90.13.4.158). The huge influx of Italian immigrants to Mulberry Bend left thousands homeless and forced to sleep in illegal lodging houses for "five cents a spot." This room and an adjoining one held fifteen men and women and a week-old baby. Riis took the photograph on a midnight expedition with the sanitary police who reported overcrowding. In his autobiography, he explained, "When the report was submitted to the Health Board the next day, it did not make much of an impression—these things rarely do, put in mere words—until my negatives, still dripping from the dark-room, came to reinforce them. From them there was no appeal."

"Knee-Pants" at Forty-five Cents a Dozen—A Ludlow Street Sweater's Shop, 1890 (90.13.4.151). Riis devoted a chapter of *How the Other Half Lives* to "the sweaters of Jewtown," who served as middlemen in the clothing business centered in the Tenth Ward on the Lower East Side. The sweaters hired recent immigrants to work at sewing machines in tenements for as many as sixteen hours a day and as little as two dollars a week, all in violation of factory labor laws. Riis visited the sweatshop with a Yiddish-speaking guide. In this photograph, the workers are "learners" who had "come over" only a few weeks earlier.

"I Scrubs," Katie Who Keeps House in West 49th Street, 1892 (90.13.4.132). To prepare *Children of the Poor*, the 1892 sequel to *How the Other Half Lives*, Riis photographed and interviewed several children. The integration of conversing and photographing produced individual portraits, very unlike the photographs of the earlier work, which were usually taken without rapport between photographer and subject.

When Riis met nine-year-old Katie at the 52nd Street Industrial School, he asked what kind of work she did, and she answered, "I scrubs." Katie and her three older siblings took their own apartment after their mother died and their father remarried. The older children worked in a hammock factory, and Katie kept house. When asked if she would pose for this picture, Katie "got right up . . . without a question and without a smile."

Minding the Baby, 1892 (90.13.4.191). Young children were often asked to "mind the baby" while their mothers worked outside the home. This photograph shows a "little mother" with a baby in a Cherry Hill tenement yard. The household goods surrounding them suggests that someone, perhaps their family, was moving in or out of the tenement. To simplify the story, the surrounding objects were cropped out when the image was published in *Children of the Poor*.

"Slept in that Cellar Four Years," 1892 (90.13.4.207). In *Children of the Poor*, Riis described visiting a Ludlow Street tenement where three peddlers lived in a "moldy cellar [with] the water . . . ankle deep on the mud floor." "It was an awful place, and by the light of my candle the three, with their unkempt beards and hair and sallow faces, looked more like hideous ghosts than living men. They had slept there among and upon decaying fruit and wreckage for over three years."

A Scrub and Her Bed—The Plank, 1892 (90.13.4.236). Police station lodging rooms, which lacked light, ventilation, or beds, were the only shelters available to the homeless in Riis's day. In the winter of 1891 to 1892, Riis toured nine police stations, which he called "a parody of municipal charity," and wrote articles advocating their replacement with wayfarers' lodges like those in Boston, which provided a bath, a clean bed, and breakfast. This photograph shows an alcoholic woman who slept upon a plank in the Eldridge Street station. A "scrub" was a beggar who worked for orthodox Jews on the Sabbath.

Old Barney in Cat Alley, 1898 (90.13.4.297). Riis took very few photographs after 1895, perhaps because he was occupied with governmental responsibilities during the anti-Tammany mayoralty of William L. Strong (1896–98). He returned to the camera at least one more time to photograph Old Barney, a retired locksmith and Civil War veteran, who lived in an attic room in Cat Alley near Riis's Mulberry Street office. When the alley was torn down for the widening of Elm (now Lafayette) Street, Riis wrote an article for *Century Magazine* about Barney, who refused to leave his home, despite the demolition. When the roof was ripped off the house, Barney finally moved out, dragging a trunk behind him. Riis saw him only once more, "key-ring in hand . . . looking fixedly at what had once been the passageway to the alley."

FIGURE 2.8 Jacob Riis, Richard Hoe Lawrence, and Henry G. Piffard, "The Tramp," 1887–88, modern print from vintage negative, Jacob A. Riis Collection, MCNY, 90.13.4.94.

the cooperation of the residents, who stood still facing the camera. By contrast, the instantaneous flashlight photographs—such as those of women "waked by flashlight" in the 30th Street station lodging house and of opium smokers oblivious to the flash—are virtually uncontrolled; the photographer entered a dark room and

FIGURE 2.9 Jacob Riis, Richard Hoe Lawrence, and Henry G. Piffard, 1887–88, "The Tramp," lantern slide, Jacob A. Riis Collection, MCNY, 90.13.2.50. As a rule, Lawrence and Piffard placed the main subject in the center of the composition to allow for the losses on all sides in the lantern slide format. Compare *Figure 2.8.*

saw very little before the moment of exposure [*Figure 2.7*]. These latter images, which account for approximately one-fourth of the total, captured what had never been seen before in a photograph. They retain their power today because the harsh light and haphazard compositions convey the chaos of living in poverty.

In no instance was the photographer able to dwell on the subtleties of composition. When his subjects faced the camera, he could not expect their prolonged cooperation, and when he worked indoors with flashlight, he was literally in the dark. The staged photographs, such as "The Tramp," tend to be static and predictable with the subjects filling the center of the frame [*Figure 2.8*]. The lantern slide process itself required this centering. When a 5 x 4-inch negative was contact printed onto a $4\frac{1}{4}$ x $3\frac{1}{4}$-inch piece of glass, the edges of the image were automatically lost. To allow room at the top and bottom of the slide for label information meant cropping the image still further into a 3 x $3\frac{1}{8}$-inch window [*Figure 2.9*]. As a result, the photographer's compositional goal was simply to ensure that the principal subject was centered. This required not artistic sensibility but technical competence, and in Lawrence and Piffard, Riis secured the competence he needed.

The January 1888 lecture marked a turning point in Riis's life, while for Lawrence and Piffard the episode was a passing fancy.[20] As Riis later wrote, "I had made out by the flashlight possibilities my companions little dreamed of."

How the Other Half Lives

Riis's lecture converted a members' meeting into a familiar public event. By the 1880s, lantern slide exhibitions, featuring travel, scientific, and religious topics, were a common form of genteel entertainment. They were held in schools, churches, theaters, and concert halls for audiences who shunned vulgar melodramas and musical variety shows, although musical accompaniment was standard. Successful lecturers attained celebrity status and crisscrossed the nation, their schedules booked by speakers' bureaus. John L. Stoddard, the most acclaimed travel lecturer of the day, commanded a fee of $250 for a lecture and attracted large crowds to prestigious venues like New York's Chickering Hall. In the pre–Civil War era, lantern slides were hand drawn, but by the mid-1870s most slides were photographic, and manufacturers specialized in stereopticons and slides sets, sometimes with accompanying scripts. Lecturers were performers who needed no special knowledge of photography.

Recognizing the opportunity to enter this field, Riis began to seek other venues for his "lay sermon," especially in the city's churches. Only ten days after his society lecture, a Long Island paper announced that "at an early date" Riis would deliver his lecture in the Congregational Church of Richmond Hill, where he was deacon. To his great disappointment, however, the lecture never materialized, and Riis resigned from his post in protest.[21] Churchmen doubted the respectability of his topic and his profession; as he later recalled, they "held the doors against Mulberry Street and the police reporter."[22]

Undaunted, Riis continued to seek credibility as a public speaker. Newspaper articles describing his willingness to speak identified him as "the deacon-reporter" to inspire public trust.[23] In late February, with the support of A.T. Schauffler, superintendent of the New York City Mission Society, Riis was invited to address the Broadway Tabernacle, where influential, socially concerned clergymen Charles Parkhurst and Josiah Strong were among the audience. Ensuring that "nothing is thrown upon the canvas that could shock the taste of any in the audience," Schauffler also arranged three appearances at prestigious uptown churches, although two of the three were canceled.[24] In March, Riis lectured at the Jamaica Opera House on Long Island, where a coronet played "Where Is My Wandering Boy Tonight?" when "Street Arabs in Night Quarters" filled the screen, and two musicians entertained during intermission.[25] In May, he spoke in New Bedford, Massachusetts, where he inspired listeners to donate twenty dollars for the Children's Aid Society to send an orphan out west to escape poverty. A reviewer, however, complained that Riis was difficult to follow because of his "German" accent and "peculiar, rasping voice."[26]

That same month, when Rev. Lyman Abbott invited him to speak at Plymouth Church in Brooklyn, Riis entered the realm of New York's clerical and charitable elite. Abbott had recently assumed the pulpit of the late Henry Ward Beecher, a renowned reformer who regularly attracted crowds of 2,500 to his Sunday sermons. Abbott also arranged a lecture at the YMCA Hall sponsored by the Charity Organization Society and asked Riis to write two articles on the tenement problem, which appeared the following year in the *Christian Union*, a weekly founded by Beecher.[27]

As Riis gained credibility, he lost money. Because Lawrence had kept the lantern slides from the first lecture, Riis commissioned another set from A.D. Fisk, a professional photographer and a subscribing member of the Society of Amateur Photographers.[28] To cover his initial costs of $219.69, which included the slides, a camera, a stereopticon, and a lawyer's fee, Riis borrowed money from William L. Craig, a friend who was a clerk in the Health Department. He divided the proceeds of his lectures with the host organization and with Schauffler and Craig, leaving little for himself. The Broadway Tabernacle lecture grossed $143.50, none of which Riis received, and other venues took in far less; the YMCA lecture collected nine dollars and New Bedford only seven.[29] For a man with four children and sizable debts—Riis had borrowed money in 1886 to build a suburban home—the lecture circuit proved financially unrewarding.

Riis was as eager to appear in print as at a lectern. In February 1888, three news stories appeared about Riis's slum outings, each of which required his close cooperation. The articles—the *New York Sun*'s "Flashes from the Slums"; the *New York Morning Journal*'s "Visible Darkness, New York's Underside Flashed on the Camera"; and *Metropolitan*'s shortened version of the *New York Sun* article—were more entertaining than uplifting; they offered their readers simple line engravings made from Riis's photographs accompanied by his colorful commentary.[30] Most remarkable was Riis's decision to copyright the title page of a book. At the top of the page, Riis placed quotations marks around the familiar expression "One Half the World does not know how the other Half Lives," and beneath it he positioned the title of his lecture,

"The Other Half, How It Lives and Dies in New York." Below, he added a titillating description: "With one hundred illustrations, photographs from real life, of the haunts of poverty and vice in the great city." Below his name, Riis noted his professional expertise as "police reporter of the New York Tribune and the Associated Press at Police Headquarters," connecting the proposed book to popular "sunshine and shadow" books, in which a "detective" guided the reader through the slums.

Riis also tried in vain to convince a national publication to run a story based on his slum photographs. Although the technology of the flashlight was new, Riis's imagery was not. Since the 1860s, *Harper's Weekly* and *Frank Leslie's Illustrated Weekly* had been publishing articles on New York's tenement fires, beer dives, police station lodging houses, sweatshops, and new immigrants. Editors assigned artists to illustrate these articles with "sketches from life," which were reproduced as fine-line wood engravings. In 1872, *Frank Leslie's* ran a four-part article, "The Homeless Poor—How the Other Half of the World Lives," at a time when Riis himself was homeless. As immigration increased and slum overcrowding intensified, these articles became more prominent; they appeared most often in August, when the summer heat increased health risks, and at Christmas, when charity was encouraged. In 1888, *Harper's* ran a cover story on a Chinese barber at 22 Mott Street who kept opium smokers in his shop, and *Frank Leslie's* ran "Election Day in New York," which depicted a policeman searching for illegally registered voters in a cheap lodging house not unlike Happy Jack's Palace [*Figures 2.7 and 2.10–2.12*].[31]

FIGURE 2.10 " 'An Ear Shave,' Snatched from Life in the Chinese Quarter of New York by Fred Barnard," *Harper's Weekly*, March 10, 1888, cover. Compare *Figure 2.7* (page 140).

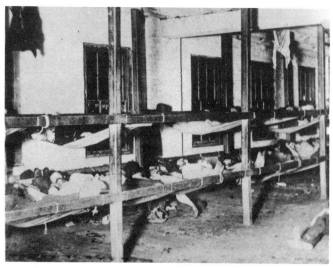

FIGURE 2.11 Jacob Riis, Richard Hoe Lawrence, and Henry G. Piffard, "Seven Cent Lodging House," 1887–88, modern print from vintage negative, Jacob A. Riis Collection, MCNY, 90.13.4.327. Riis had a copy negative made from a print because the original negative was lost or broken.

FIGURE 2.12 "Incidents of an Election in New York City—Looking for Colonizers in a Cheap Lodging House," *Frank Leslie's Illustrated Newspaper*, November 10, 1888, 208. General Research Division, the New York Public Library, Astor, Lenox and Tilden Foundation. Compare *Figure 2.11*.

Henry Harper of *Harper's Weekly* expressed interest in a Riis article, but the editor to whom Riis was referred wanted only to buy the photographs. When the editor offered to "find a man who could write" to tell the story, Riis took offense, and they parted without "mutual expressions of esteem."[32]

Turned down by the illustrated weeklies, Riis eventually reached a national audience in *Scribner's Magazine*, a "quality" monthly aimed at upper-middle-class readers. A *Scribner's* editor who had heard Riis lecture gave him twenty pages in the magazine's 1889 Christmas issue. The small adjustment to Riis's title—from "The Other Half, How It Lives and Dies in New York" to "How the Other Half Lives, Studies Among the Tenements"—reflected the more genteel atmosphere of the monthly magazines. By deleting "and Dies," the title became less sensational; by deleting "New York," it became less local; and by adding "studies," it became more picturesque.

Riis's text was distilled from his lectures and skillfully combined sensationalism and sermonizing. He began with a history lesson, which described how New York's rapid growth created "the tenement, the Frankenstein of our city civilization." He then led his reader from the elevated station at Franklin Square, through the Fourth Ward to Mulberry Bend, into Chinatown, and across the Bowery to the Jewish quarter. He related his encounters with girls addicted to opium and with a child whose family had been killed in a tenement fire. He described stock characters, such as the "tramp," who thought the world owed him a living, and the "tough," who had "some of the qualities that would go toward making a hero under different training and social conditions." And he championed the cause of social reform: "It is manifest that all effort to reclaim [the tough's] kind must begin with the conditions of life against which his very existence is a protest." Although "and Dies" had been deleted from the article's title, Riis concluded by noting the final irony of tenement life: "In the common trench of the Poor Burying Ground they lie packed three stories deep, shoulder to shoulder, crowded in earth as they were in life to 'save space.' "[33]

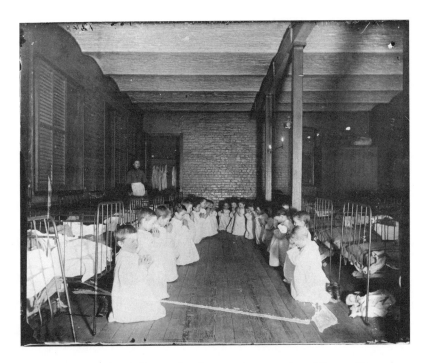

FIGURE 2.13 Jacob Riis and unknown photographer, "Prayer-Time in the Nursery—Five Points House of Industry," 1887–88, modern print from vintage negative, Jacob A. Riis Collection, MCNY, 90.13.4.127.

By late 1889, Riis had been out with his own camera for almost two years, and ten of the article's eighteen photographic illustrations were his new work. All of the photographs depicted tenement life, except for the sentimental charity scene "Prayer-Time in the Nursery—Five Points House of Industry," which was taken by the second of the two professional photographers Riis hired before learning to use the camera himself [*Figure 2.13*].[34] The new images

FIGURE 2.14 Jacob Riis, "Street Arabs in Sleeping Quarters," 1888–89, modern print from vintage negative, Jacob A. Riis Collection, MCNY, 90.13.4.126.

included staged outdoor tableaux, such as two views of "Street Arabs in Sleeping Quarters" [*Figure 2.14*]; outdoor scenes, such as "At the Cradle of the Tenement—Doorway of an Old Fashionable Dwelling on Cherry Hill" [*Figure 2.15*]; and indoor instantaneous photographs, such as "Lodgers in a Crowded Bayard Street Tenement—'Five Cents a Spot'" [*Figure 2.16*] and "An All-Night Two-Cent Restaurant in 'The Bend'" [*Figure 2.17*].

FIGURE 2.15 Jacob Riis, "At the Cradle of the Tenement—Doorway of an Old Fashionable Dwelling on Cherry Hill," 1888–89, modern print from vintage negative, Jacob A. Riis Collection, MCNY, 90.13.4.101.

FIGURE 2.16 Jacob Riis, "Lodgers in a Crowded Bayard Street Tenement—'Five Cents a Spot,'" 1888–89, modern print from vintage negative, Jacob A. Riis Collection, MCNY, 90.13.4.158.

FIGURE 2.17 Jacob Riis, "An All-Night Two-Cent Restaurant in 'The Bend,'" 1888–89, modern print from vintage negative, Jacob A. Riis Collection, MCNY, 90.13.4.107.

The illustrations of Riis's photographs in the *Scribner's* article did not look like photographs, nor did *Scribner's* describe them as such. For twelve of the illustrations, *Scribner's* used fine-line wood engravings based upon photographs, the standard reproduction technique of the time. Five artists made pen-and-ink drawings from the photographs, which were then transferred to woodblocks and engraved by craftsmen. The photographs were not copied literally; the artists corrected flattened perspective, eliminated out-of-focus areas, and

FIGURE 2.18 Otto H. Bacher, "At the Cradle of the Tenement—
Doorway of an Old Fashioned Dwelling on Cherry Hill," *Scribner's
Magazine*, December 1889, 644. Compare the wood engraving made
from Bacher's drawing with Riis's original photograph, *Figure 2.15*.

added narrative incident. The artist Otto H. Bacher, for example,
faithfully retained the architectural background of Riis's photograph
of a Cherry Street doorway but freely rearranged the figures to make
a more coherent composition [*Figure 2.18*]. He eliminated two of
the figures, brought two others closer to the center where he placed
them face to face, and added a pair of children in the doorway.

Of the artists, only Kenyon Cox was relatively loyal to the originals. In "Lodgers in a Crowded Bayard Street Tenement—'Five

FIGURE 2.19 Kenyon Cox, "Lodgers in a Crowded Bayard Street Tenement— 'Five Cents a Spot,' " *Scribner's Magazine*, December 1889, 650. Compare the wood engraving made after Cox's drawing with the original photograph, *Figure 2.16*.

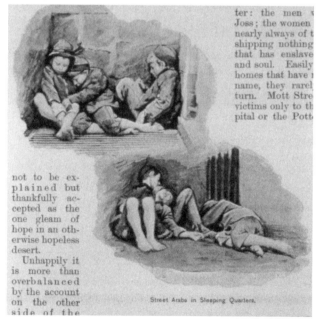

FIGURE 2.20 "Street Arabs in Sleeping Quarters," *Scribner's Magazine*, December 1889, 655. Compare the halftone after the original photograph, *Figure 2.14*.

ter: the men Joss; the women nearly always of t shipping nothing that has enslave and soul. Easily homes that have name, they rarel turn. Mott Stre victims only to th pital or the Pott

not to be ex-plained but thankfully ac-cepted as the one gleam of hope in an oth-erwise hopeless desert.

Unhappily it is more than overbalanced by the account on the other side of the

Street Arabs in Sleeping Quarters.

Cents a Spot,'" Cox retained the chaotic shapes of men rudely awakened by Riis's flash and included minute details, from the dark cap hanging on the wall to the shoes on the floor [*Figure 2.19*]. Next to his signature, he wrote in bold letters, "After Photo." The words may have been intended as much to disassociate Cox from the awkward, unconventional composition of Riis's photograph as to emphasize the value of the photograph as evidence.

For the other six photographic illustrations, *Scribner's* experimented with halftones, a process that it pioneered. Publishers had long sought a way to reproduce art with a full range of tones on the same page as type, and the halftone process provided a solution. The work of art was photographed through a screen, which converted the original into a pattern of dots, and the screened image was then transferred onto a metal plate and printed with ink. When the original was a photograph, the halftone process eliminated the need for copy artists and engravers. Although cost-effective, it was still a primitive technology in 1889. In "Street Arabs in Sleeping Quarters," for example, an artist had to enhance the gray, flat image by strengthening the contours, adding highlights, and eliminating the dull areas that surrounded the figures [*Figure 2.20*]. The end result looked more like a wash drawing than a photograph.

Scribner's added three wood engravings made from artists' sketches to the photographic illustrations, further blurring the distinction between photograph and drawing. Riis tolerated W.T. Fitler's two overhead views of pushcarts in the Jewish quarter, but Victor Perard's "Coffee at One Cent" provoked his ire [*Figure 2.21*].

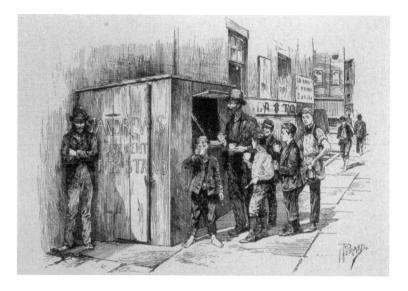

FIGURE 2.21 Victor Perard, "Coffee at One Cent," *Scribner's Magazine*, December 1889, 658. Riis complained that this wood engraving made from a drawing by Perard "was not mine and had nothing to do with [the story]."

On his copy of the article, he scribbled: "This picture was smuggled into the story. It was not mine and had nothing to do with it."[35]

The same month that the article appeared, Riis contracted with Charles Scribner's Sons to convert it into a book. Writing at night for a year, he expanded each component of the article—the historical introduction, the tour, and the call to action—into a 300-page volume entitled *How the Other Half Lives*. With the assistance of Dr. Roger S. Tracy of the Health Department, he laced the text with statistics on population growth, disease, and crime. He included five floor plans and a bird's-eye view of a crowded tenement block, and reviewed recent efforts to reform tenement design. As a solution to the housing crisis, he commended the model apartments of Brooklyn builder A.T. White, who provided affordable, decent rentals to poor families and still earned a 5 percent profit. As he bolstered his argument with facts and figures, he increased its emotional intensity, seeking to arouse his readers by appealing to their fear of disease and political unrest as well as their Christian charity. The book ended with the haunting words of poet James Russell Lowell: "Think ye that building shall endure / Which shelters the noble and crushes the poor?"

Scribner's reprinted all twenty-one illustrations that appeared in the magazine article and added seventeen new photographs: ten Lawrence/Piffard photographs, five Riis photographs, and two photographs acquired from other sources. All but two of the new photographs were reproduced as full-page halftones, measuring $3\frac{1}{2}$ by $4\frac{1}{2}$ inches.[36] Unlike the heavily reworked images of the article, the new halftones were relatively untouched. In the "Bandit's Roost" halftone, for example, an artist enhanced the woman and small children on the left edge, who are barely visible in the negative, but the image looks like a photograph and not a drawing [*Figure 2.22*].

The style of the new images reflected the improvements in the halftone process from the previous year. Something more, however, seemed to have occurred. Not only did the new images look like photographs, but Scribner's touted them as such. The title page announced that the book was illustrated "chiefly from photographs taken by the author." By not masking the disorienting graphic qualities of the photographs, the publisher encouraged readers to experience them as proof of the deplorable social conditions that Riis was seeking to improve.

How the Other Half Lives was a colossal bestseller, remaining in print throughout Riis's lifetime. Riis's scrapbook contains more than eighty reviews from newspapers across the country, which are virtually unanimous in their praise. In 1891, Samson and Low Company published a London edition, and in 1892 Scribner's issued a less expensive American edition. Puzzled by the book's extraordinary success, Riis mused, "Perhaps it was that I had had it in me so long that it burst out at last with a rush that caught on."[37]

The publication that same year of William Booth's *In Darkest England and The Way Out* gave reviewers a convenient basis for comparison. General Booth, as he was called, was a Methodist missionary who had worked in London's East End for forty years and founded the Salvation Army. His book, which appeared shortly after his popular American lecture tour, described London's poverty and his remedies for it. Taking his title from Henry Morton Stanley's *In Darkest Africa*, Booth suggested that London's poor were as isolated from the rest of society as the Africans whom Stanley found in the Congo. American reviewers extended the analogy, calling Riis's book a study of "darkest New York."

The differences between the two books help explain Riis's success. Booth's tone was sanctimonious and doleful, and his remedies, which included mass emigration, were quixotic. Riis, by contrast, wrote in the lively style of a seasoned journalist; he focused on one

BANDITS' ROOST.

FIGURE 2.22 "Bandit's Roost," *How the Other Half Lives* (New York: Charles Scribner's Sons, 1890), 63. Scribner's used all the illustrations from the magazine article and added fifteen full-page halftones.

problem, the tenement; and he proposed practical solutions. The *Chicago Tribune* commended Riis for "depict[ing] faithfully without the exaggerated zeal of a philanthromaniac, but with the calm, critical spirit of a close observer."[38] The *Epoch* noted that Riis's book was "not the vaporing of a visionary, but the experience of a newspaper reporter."[39] And the *Brooklyn Times* observed that the "book is, in fact, with all its revelations, not at all sensational, simply offering, in vigorous, humane, and fascinating narrative, the plain lineaments of truth."[40] Riis's racial characterizations—the godless Chinese, the penurious Jew, and the dirty Italian—were seen as evidence of his knowledge of the slums, not of his prejudices. "Mr. Riis takes each nationality in turn, and deals with all alike impartially," wrote the *Chicago Herald*.[41] Only the *Critic*, a New York literary journal, expressed a preference for Booth: "There is [in Riis] a lack of broad and penetrative vision, a singularly warped sense of justice at times, and a roughness amounting almost to brutality." It referred readers to "Gen. Booth's book 'In Darkest England,' where the true Christ-spirit is made manifest." The reviewer, who never mentioned Riis's photographs, disparaged Riis's book as "literally a photograph, [which] as such has its value and lesson, but also its serious limitations."[42]

It was Riis's text, not his photographic illustrations, that attracted attention. Most writers who took note of the photographs considered them as further proof of Riis's veracity. According to the *Catholic World*, "The illustration by means of photographs secures fidelity to facts and to the sad realities with which the book deals."[43] The *Christian Intelligencer* similarly observed that "the photographs taken by [the author] . . . actualize to the reader the real state of things, and deepen the impression on his mind."[44] No one suggested that the photographs were artistic or revolutionary. Riis's own paper, the *Evening Sun,* concluded that "while there is not much to be said for [the photographs'] artistic merit, there is something very unusual, not to say interesting, in looking in at midnight with the unerring eye of the 'Kodak.' "[45] The *Sunday School Times* was even more blunt: it noted that the volume was "illustrated by poorly printed pictures from instantaneous photographs."[46]

The Children of the Poor

In May 1891, Riis told the *Brooklyn Times* that he did "not believe in following a popular book with another written simply to meet an assumed demand" and would wait "until he had a subject that impelled him as strongly as the subject of [his] first success."[47] By that fall, he was working on *Children of the Poor*, which appeared in May 1892 as an article in *Scribner's Magazine* and in October 1892 as a 300-page book. Scribner's conceived the new book as a sequel to *How the Other Half Lives*—the two books were designed identically—as did Riis; in the preface he wrote, "The two books are one. Each supplements the other."

Children of the Poor, which Riis dedicated to his own children whom he hoped would "carry forward the work," grew out of his personal experience. In 1888, not long after he had moved from Brooklyn to Richmond Hill, Riis's three young children brought him armfuls of daisies to take to "the poors." The city children "went wild over the 'posies,' " and when Riis had no more flowers to give them, he "sat in the gutter and wept with grief." Riis wrote a column asking New York commuters to bring in flowers for the city's poor children, and to his amazement his office was overrun with boxes and barrels of blooms. During the flower campaign, he met the King's Daughters, a missionary organization, and began a lifelong association with the group. In 1890, the King's Daughters opened a settlement house in a Madison Street tenement, which in 1901 moved to Henry Street and was renamed the Jacob A. Riis Settlement.[48] It was his efforts on behalf of the settlement that put Riis in regular contact with the philanthropic agencies working with children in the poorest neighborhoods.[49]

Riis's views on child welfare were more hopeful than his gloomy outlook on tenement reform. His optimism was due to his faith in the resilience of children and to the dramatic increase in philanthropic activity. The first half of *Children of the Poor* describes inadequate public schools, child labor in factories and sweatshops, the lack of playgrounds and parks, and homelessness and is told through the vivid stories of children whom Riis interviewed and sometimes photographed. The second half of the book describes the pioneer work of the Children's Aid Society (founded in 1852), the Society for the Prevention of Cruelty to Children (founded in 1874), and the more recently organized settlement houses, kindergartens, industrial schools, and boys' clubs. An appendix lists the addresses of more than 270 programs serving New York City's needy children.

Although Riis prided himself on presenting facts, not theories, he offered strong opinions about the political implications of poverty and placed his hopes in the process of Americanization. Bitterly opposed to Tammany's control of immigrants' votes, he declared that "the problem of the children is the problem of the State." He believed that America's future depended upon making "useful citizens" of the "children of the toiling masses in the cities," and he countered the racial fears of his middle-class readers with a vision of upward mobility and responsible citizenship:

> Yesterday it was the swarthy Italian, to-day the Russian Jew, that excited our distrust. . . . All alike they have taken, or are taking, their places in the ranks of our social phalanx, pushing upward from the bottom with steady effort, as I believe they will continue to do. . . . And in the general advance the children, thus firmly grasped, are . . . a powerful moving force.[50]

The *Scribner's* article was loosely written and anecdotal, focusing primarily on Riis's firsthand encounters. The reader was introduced to "little toilers" like nine-year-old Katie, who cooked and cleaned house for her three older siblings so they could work in a hammock factory; thirteen-year-old Pietro, who was crippled by a streetcar accident but was learning to read and write English; and nine-year-old Edward, an orphan who earned his living hailing customers for a peddler. The book version was more tightly organized and detailed than the article and was enlivened by more portraits. Among the new characters were Little Susie of Gotham Court, "whose picture [Riis] took while she was pasting linen on tin covers

FIGURE 2.23 Jacob Riis, " 'I Scrubs,' Little Katie from the West 52nd Street Industrial School," 1890–92, modern print from vintage nega-tive, Jacob A. Riis Collection, MCNY, 90.13.4.132.

for pocket-flasks . . . with hands so deft and swift that even the flash could not catch her moving arm," and Tommy, a bootblack who was "a hopeless young scamp" but "so aggravatingly funny that it was impossible not to laugh."

By the time Riis was photographing for *Children of the Poor*, he had learned to use the camera as an extension of his interviews.

FIGURE 2.24 Jacob Riis, "Little Susie in Gotham Court," 1890–92, modern print from vintage negative, Jacob A. Riis Collection, MCNY, 90.13.4.133.

When photographing Katie at the 52nd Street Industrial School, he got his title, "I Scrubs," when he asked her what kind of work she did [*Figure 2.23*]. She stood for her picture "without a question and without a smile" but later invited Riis to her home on West 49th Street, which he found "all clean, if poor."[51] Riis met Pietro at the Mulberry Street police station, where the boy was "interpreting for

FIGURE 2.25 Jacob Riis, "Night-School; in the Seventh Avenue Lodging House—Edward, the Little Peddler, Caught Napping," 1890–92, modern print from vintage negative, Jacob A. Riis Collection, MCNY, 90.13.4.173.

the defense in a shooting case," and Riis convinced him to be photographed with his family in their Jersey Street home. Little Susie was photographed "at work" in her Gotham Court home [*Figure 2.24*], and Edward, who refused to be photographed at work, was photographed asleep at his desk in an evening-school class at the Seventh Avenue Lodging House [*Figure 2.25*]. It was in pursuit

FIGURE 2.26 Jacob Riis, "A Ludlow Street Sweater's Shop," 1888–89, modern print from vintage negative, Jacob A. Riis Collection, MCNY, 90.13.4.151.

of photographing Edward that Riis met Tommy the bootblack. Although there is nothing special about the composition of these photographs, they reflect Riis's growing comfort with the camera as a research tool.

A comparison of photographs from *How the Other Half Lives* with those of *Children of the Poor* demonstrates the change in

FIGURE 2.27 Jacob Riis, "Minding the Baby, Cherry Hill," 1890–92, modern print from vintage negative, Jacob A. Riis Collection, MCNY, 90.13.4.191.

FIGURE 2.28 Jacob Riis, "Slept in That Cellar Four Years," 1890–92, modern print from vintage negative, Jacob A. Riis Collection, MCNY, 90.13.4.207.

Riis's photographic practice. "A Ludlow Street Sweater's Shop," for example, which appears in the first book, depicts the moment Riis entered the room: "The boy and the woman alone look up at our entrance. . . . The men do not appear to be aware even of the presence of a stranger." Riis photographed before he established rapport with his subjects [*Figure 2.26*]. Only afterward did his

FIGURE 2.29 Jacob Riis, "The First Board of Election in the Beach Street Industrial School," 1890–92, modern print from vintage negative, Jacob A. Riis Collection, MCNY, 90.13.4.169.

Yiddish-speaking guide help him conduct an extensive interview in which the "wife of the boss . . . disinclined to talk at first . . . gr[e]w almost talkative."[52] As he grew more confident with the mechanics of the camera, however, Riis waited and learned to use the camera more naturally. His photographs in *Children of the Poor* display this increased level of trust between subject and photographer. In

"Minding the Baby," which illustrates the common practice of leaving babies in the care of young girls while their mothers went to work, the "little mother" posed naturally for Riis and smiled for the camera [*Figure 2.27*]. Similarly, Riis captured the dignity of a peddler who "slept in the mouldy cellar [of a Ludlow Street tenement], where the water was ankle deep on the mud floor" [*Figure 2.28*]. That he "had occasion to visit [the tenement] repeatedly," perhaps on behalf of the King's Daughters, may have helped him develop a rapport with the peddler.

Riis also discovered a way to use photographs emblematically. In researching his chapter on industrial schools, he discovered at the Beach Street Industrial School a potent symbol of Americanization—saluting the flag. *Children of the Poor* included three photographs of aspects of this "unique exercise . . . that la[id] hold of the very marrow of the problem": the election to initiate the salute; a group portrait of the board of electors, which consisted of an Irish, an African American, and an Italian child [*Figure 2.29*]; and the salute itself, which became the book's frontispiece.

Although Riis had developed his photographic technique, his publisher seems not to have noticed. Scribner's ignored the tighter integration of narrative and text, making no effort to insert the illustrations near the text that described them. In some instances, the result was awkward, as in the case of Tommy the bootblack, who is discussed on page 268, where the reader is directed to his picture "on page 100." Scribner's simply repeated the same production strategies for the second article and book that it had used for the first.

MINDING THE BABY.

FIGURE 2.30 Jacob Riis, "Minding the Baby," *Children of the Poor* (New York: Scribner's and Sons, 1892), 114. In its second book by Riis, Scribner's instructed an engraver to outline the figures in the halftone plates to make them more legible. Compare *Figure 2.22* from *How the Other Half Lives* (page 161).

The magazine assigned artists to copy Riis's photographs, which were then reproduced as either wood engravings or heavily manipulated halftones.[53] In producing the book-length version of *Children of the Poor*, Scribner's used all the illustrations from the article and added others, which were reproduced as halftones directly from photographs, without the intermediate step of an artist's drawing.[54]

It appears, however, that Scribner's may have been more wary about using Riis's photographs in the second book than in the first. The title page announced only that the book was "illustrated," not that it was "illustrated chiefly from photographs taken by the author," and none of the photographs were reproduced full page. The halftones in the second book were more heavily reworked than in the first: the major forms were distinctly outlined, which enhanced their clarity but lessened their photographic appearance [*Figure 2.30*]. Perhaps Scribner's was reacting to the criticism that *How the Other Half Lives* was "illustrated by poorly printed pictures from instantaneous photographs." It was attracted to the cost-effectiveness of using halftones made directly from photographs but was struggling with the aesthetic risks of the new, still primitive medium.

The reviews of *Children of the Poor* were universally positive but, once again, the illustrations attracted little attention. At the conclusion of its lengthy review, the *New York Tribune* mentioned that "frequent illustrations enforce vividly the lessons of the text," and the *New York Sun* incorrectly noted that "Mr. Riis works with pencil and camera both, and the complete results of his labors are here included." The *Critic* cited the "abundant illustrations which take hold of the heart as well as the eye."

Most writers commended Riis's investigative rigor and lack of sentimentality. The *Brooklyn Times*, for example, noted that the book presented its subject "not in the sentimental outlines of the goody story book, but as they actually are . . . with much candor and sympathy."[55] Riis recalled about his second book that "critics said there were more 'bones' in it," noting the specificity of its research and practical nature of its policy recommendations, such as the use of birth certificates to enforce child labor laws.[56]

Reviewers also applauded Riis's optimism. "The earlier book was sad beyond expression, for it told only of wretchedness and woe; the new one has in it gleams of a brighter day," wrote the *Charities Review*.[57] Some credited Riis's ability to understand the strength and courage of poor children to his own experience of poverty. The *San Francisco Chronicle* wrote: "[The book] reveals pity for lost opportunities, but it also shows that the poor possess a certain proud independence which those who are born to the purple of wealth never understand." The *Christian Register* considered *Children of the Poor* "a better book than its predecessor [because] it seems to have been written out of a steadier purpose and a deeper sympathy." Steering clear of "the offensive and corrupting descriptions of wickedness such as have been too commonly connected with the work of 'moral reform,'" the book also offered "no forced note of sympathy, no cant, pretence, or humbug."[58] In "Heredity and Poverty," a long review in the *New York Tribune*, Riis's optimism was interpreted as a refutation of racial theories of moral behavior: "If a careful comparison of the data furnished in different chapters is correct and is rightly understood, this evidence shows that the moral quality of the individual has nothing to do with the race from which he sprang, but is wholly a personal tendency due to training, good or bad, as the case may be, from childhood."[59] Although Riis favored practical solutions over theoretical debate, he saved two copies of this review.

Despite positive critical response, *Children of the Poor* was not a sensation like its predecessor. As the first book ran through printings, the second book's sales remained flat. *Children of the Poor* no doubt suffered because it was a sequel. Its more temperate tone and message may have disappointed readers, who preferred the picturesque slum tour and threat of political upheaval in *How the Other Half Lives* to its individualized portraits and progress report.

The 1890s:
Riis's Last Photographs

Riis's most active years as a photographer were 1891 and 1892, while he was preparing *Children of the Poor*. In addition to compiling new images for the book, he took photographs to illustrate numerous newspaper articles, primarily for the *Evening Sun*, where he remained on staff until 1899, and for magazine articles. After 1892, as his fame grew and other demands on his time increased, Riis's use of the camera waned. His lecture tours became national in scope, he published a volume of Christmas stories,[60] and with the 1895 election of Mayor William Strong he took a minor but active role in reform government. In 1894 and 1895, Riis hired two photographers to work for him, and between 1895 and 1898 his own photography dwindled to a handful of images a year.[61]

FIGURE 2.31 Jacob Riis, "James M'Bride, One of the City's Pensioners," 1889, modern print from vintage negative, Jacob A. Riis Collection, MCNY, 90.13.4.98.

As early as 1889, Riis began taking photographs for specific newspaper articles. In July of that year, the *Evening Sun* printed "The Blind See To-Day," which reported on the annual pilgrimage of the city's indigent blind to receive their pensions [*Figure 2.31*].[62] "It is the blind beggars' pay day," Riis explained, "and this day of all in the year one shall look in vain through the streets of New York for the familiar figure at the corner lamp post with the handful of rubber-tipped pencils held out beseechingly." To illustrate the article, Riis photographed "James M'Bride, One of the City's Pensioners," standing against a lamppost, box of pencils in hand, face tilted "beseechingly" upward.

In April 1891, a long article on Smallpox Island, which praised the city's newly built hospital and the devotion of its staff, was illustrated with six "pictures from photographs taken by me," as Riis noted in his scrapbook.[63] And in June, "The City's Unclaimed Dead," which traced the pauper's route from the city's morgue and charity hospitals to Potter's Field on Hart's Island, was illustrated with five engravings after "photographs taken by me."[64]

These stories, which offered glimpses of the life of the poor, were similar to those Riis had written for years, and their photographs were meant to inform, not provoke fear or disgust. Shortly thereafter, however, Riis launched three public health initiatives in which he used photographs to arouse strong emotions and force governmental action. In August, he created a cause célèbre by exposing dangerous pollution of the Croton Reservoir, the source of New York City's water supply.[65] Noticing "a trace of nitrites" in the Board of Health's weekly water analysis, Riis "sounded the warning in [his] paper" and spent a week "following to its source every stream that discharged into the Croton River and photographing [his] evidence wherever [he] found it." His photographs depict at water's edge "chicken killeries," outhouses, stables, two public dumps, and a condensed milk factory previously cited by the Health Department for drawing

Chicken Killeries & Hotel outhouses on shore of Lake Mahopac

FIGURE 2.32 Jacob Riis, "Chicken Killeries and Hotel Outhouses on Shore of Lake Mahopac," August 1891. Riis's water pollution negatives are lost. He pasted eleven prints in his scrapbook, of which this is one. Jacob A. Riis Papers, Library of Congress.

milk from cows infected with tuberculosis" [*Figure 2.32*].[66] Writing several articles in a two-week period, Riis set in motion a political uproar that resulted, the following winter, in the city's purchasing land on the banks of the Croton River to protect the water.

In 1892, while investigating the murder of a girl at the Rutgers Street dump on the Lower East Side, Riis encountered a colony of

Italian ragpickers living along the waterfront in shelters created by the wooden overhangs where scows dumped the city's refuse. The discovery spawned his second public health initiative. Combing through the ash-covered garbage, Italian immigrants had turned the dumps into a business, collecting for resale rags, bones, tin cans, glass, paper, scrap metal, and hats. Two years earlier, the Health Department had ordered the ragpickers to evacuate the dumps and had required them to wash rags before reselling them. Observing that both orders had been ignored, Riis decided to survey the city's sixteen waterside dumps; he examined eleven, five of which he photographed, and solicited reports on the remaining five. On March 18, 1892, his *Evening Sun* article, "Real Wharf Rats," revealed the filthy conditions in which the ragpickers lived and worked, and reported that rags were being returned unwashed to rag shops from the city's ash barrels. In September, fear of cholera led the Board of Health to reinvestigate the dumps.

Despite its sensational subtitle, "Human Rodents That Live on Garbage Under the Wharves," Riis's article expressed an ambivalent attitude toward the dumps' inhabitants. In some passages, his judgment was harsh: "[The dump] is their only home [which] they share . . . with unfold myriads of rats and bands of frowsy, ill-favored curs, and here and there a goat, that feed with them off the refuse of the ash barrels on equal terms." In others, he was more understanding: "As the Italians work in shifts night and day . . . and need the room under the dump for storing their stuff, it will be simply impossible to drive them from their quarters there, and safer, per-

FIGURE 2.33 Jacob Riis, "Among the Offal at West 47th Street," 1892, modern print from vintage negative, Jacob A. Riis Collection, MCNY, 90.13.4.209.

haps, than to let them scatter among the tenement after their work is over." He was as concerned for the physical and moral welfare of the ragpickers as he was for public safety, and he was especially disturbed that so many young boys sacrificed their health and education to work there. Riis concluded the article with questions rather than demands: "Ought the police to let them stay? Can they drive them out at all? Some say they can't."

FIGURE 2.34 Jacob Riis, "In Sleeping Quarters—Rivington Street Dump," 1892, modern print from vintage negative, Jacob A. Riis Collection, MCNY, 90.13.4.208.

FIGURE 2.35 Jacob Riis, "A Child of the Dump," 1892, vintage print (negative lost), Jacob A. Riis Collection, MCNY, 90.13.3.116.

Riis's nine photographs for "Wharf Rats," taken at the Rivington, Rutgers, West 35th, West 38th, and West 47th Streets dumps, show people scavenging and at rest in their shelters.[67] The images underscore Riis's ambivalent attitude. In "Among the Offal at West 47th Street," for example, a man seen from a distance rooting around in garbage seems to meld into his chaotic environment [*Figure 2.33*]. In "In Sleeping Quarters—Rivington Street Dump," by contrast, a man contentedly smoking a pipe faces the camera as he sits in his makeshift but orderly home [*Figure 2.34*]. And in "A Child of the Dump," a handsome, somber boy poses for a portrait [*Figure 2.35*]. Riis included the latter two photographs, the most sympathetic of the group, in *Children of the Poor.*

Riis's third public health proposal—to close the police station lodging houses—was his most ambitious. Twenty of the city's police stations provided nightly shelter for the homeless, either in cellars or above jails at the back of the stations. Beds consisted of planks placed on iron racks, and in winter the vermin-infested, unventilated rooms were regularly overcrowded. Riis opposed these shelters because they were dangerous and degrading as well as breeding grounds for disease. In their stead, he advocated the adoption of the "Boston Plan," where municipal lodges provided a clean bed, shower, and a decent meal in exchange for a morning's work. "[The plan] does not solve the tramp question, but it solves the question who are the tramps . . . —who by choice will work— . . . and who not."[68]

In January and February 1892, Riis published two illustrated articles on the police station lodging houses. The first reported on the tour of the slums by Lady Henry Somerset, a distinguished London reformer, and the second on a petition by a group of charitable organizations to the Board of Health to "mak[e] an immediate inspection in order so that the facts may be officially ascertained and . . . the necessary remedy be applied without delay." After a year of inaction, a case of typhus was found in the Eldridge Street

FIGURE 2.36 Jacob Riis, "Women's Lodging Room in West 47th Street Station," 1892, modern print from vintage negative, Jacob A. Riis Collection, MCNY, 90.13.4.208.

station house, which stimulated two more Riis articles and a lantern slide presentation at the Academy of Medicine.[69] Even when typhus broke out in three more police lodging houses, city hall still refused to act, and in March 1893 the Charity Organization Society responded to the crisis by opening a municipal lodge based on the Boston model.[70]

Riis's interest in this issue was personal as well as political. Shortly after his arrival in New York in 1870, he found refuge in the Church Street station house, where he was robbed of a Danish keepsake, accused of lying, and thrown into the street; when his dog growled at the policeman who had mistreated him, the policeman killed the dog. Riis recounted this brutalizing experience in his first newspaper article on the police lodging houses.[71] The story buttressed his belief that the lodgings posed a moral as well as physical threat to innocent youths, who could be corrupted by hardened "tramps" and by the police, who "heartily detest[ed] the whole business."[72]

Riis's twenty photographs of nine police lodging houses represent his most extensive documentation of a single subject. Most of the images survey an entire room to reveal various degrees of crowding and disorder. At the West 47th Street Station in Hell's Kitchen, the women's lodging room is relatively empty, with laundry strung on lines, but the women sleep directly on the dirty floor [*Figure* 2.36]. The men's lodging room is so packed with sleeping bodies and a pile of firewood in the far corner that it is difficult to distinguish between animate and inanimate forms [*Figure* 2.37]. Other than Riis's flash, the only apparent light source was a pot-bellied stove. In most images, some lodgers turn toward the camera, surprised by the momentary brightness. One of the most affecting images—the only one to include men and women together—shows a crowd on the dark stairs of the Mulberry Street Station, startled by the flash as they wait to get into the cellar rooms [*Figure* 2.38].

FIGURE 2.37 Jacob Riis, "Men's Lodging Room in West 47th Street Station," 1892, modern print from vintage negative, Jacob A. Riis Collection, MCNY, 90.13.4.234.

On several occasions, Riis enlisted lodgers to pose for him. At the Oak Street Station, he chose six young men to stand before the camera to refute conventional wisdom that the station house lodgers were broken old men. At the Church Street Station, he solicited three young men to pose for a photograph entitled, "I Slept Here," and interviewed them about their life stories [*Figure 2.39*]. By contrast, his photograph at Eldridge Street of "A Scrub

FIGURE 2.38 Jacob Riis, "Waiting to Be Let in the Mulberry Street Station," 1892, modern print from vintage negative, Jacob A. Riis Collection, MCNY, 90.13.4.230.

and Her Bed" was intended to show that the women lodgers there were old and alcoholic [*Figure 2.40*]. Explaining that a "scrub" was a woman who was hired to work for Jews on their Sabbath, Riis deemed the Eldridge Street woman a representative of this group. A photograph that was central to Riis's narrative showed the first identified typhus victim sleeping on the floor of the Eldridge Street Station [*Figure 2.41*].[73]

FIGURE 2.39 Jacob Riis, " 'I Slept Here,' Church Street Station,"
1892, modern print from vintage negative, Jacob A. Riis Collection,
MCNY, 90.13.4.229.

Riis's next foray with the camera was in the fall of 1894, when he
took photographs to illustrate three articles for *Century Magazine*,
an influential journal founded in 1881 to which he was a regular
contributor. The close friendship between Riis and Richard Watson
Gilder, the magazine's editor, dated from the 1894 Tenement
House Commission, which Gilder chaired. For "Playgrounds for

FIGURE 2.40 Jacob Riis, "A Scrub and Her Bed, Eldridge Street Station," 1892, modern print from vintage negative, Jacob A. Riis Collection, MCNY, 90.13.4.236.

City Schools," Riis photographed the condemned Essex-Market School, showing children at recess, crowded into a dark hallway with "school sinks"—toilets without plumbing—opening onto it, and classrooms so dark that gaslights had to be turned on during the day.[74] For "The Making of Thieves in New York," Riis photographed boys at the Juvenile Asylum, where the city sent truants to

FIGURE 2.41 Jacob Riis, "The Single Typhus Lodger in Eldridge Street Station," 1892, modern print from vintage negative, Jacob A. Riis Collection, MCNY, 90.13.4.247.

live alongside thieves.[75] Riis also enlisted the services of Fisk, the professional photographer who had made his lantern slides, to take twelve photographs, two of which appeared in the article.[76] For "One Way Out," Riis photographed the Hall Farm, in Kensico, New York, where the Children's Aid Society had initiated a new program to

FIGURE 2.42 Jacob Riis, "The Baby's Playground," 1888–95, modern print from vintage negative, Jacob A. Riis Collection, MCNY, 90.13.4.122.

train older city boys in farming.[77] The three articles grew naturally out of the issues Riis had discussed in *Children of the Poor.*

The next spring, the clearing of Mulberry Bend brought Riis back to his first photographic subject. "As the recognized Mulberry Bend crank," he wrote in his autobiography, "I laid in a stock of dry plates and buckled to."[78] In 1888, the city decided to purchase the decayed houses, rear tenements, and "rookeries" of Mulberry Bend (bordered by Mulberry, Park, Baxter, and Bayard Streets) and replace them with a small park. Despite the backing of social reformers, the city's leaders were reluctant to seize private property and dragged their feet until 1895, when landlords were finally compensated more than a million dollars. On the eve of demolition, Riis wrote a lengthy article for the *Evening Sun*, "Goodby to the Bend," which recounted the history of the site, chronicled many of its celebrated crimes, and described the colorful aspects of Italian street life.[79]

Riis already had a backlog of photographs of the Bend for the article, including "Bandit's Roost," "Baxter Alley," "Bottle Alley," "A Two-Cent Restaurant," and "Lodgers at Five Cents a Spot." He used three of these images, plus two previously unpublished interior views—"The Baby's Playground," which revealed a toddler standing in the filth overflowing from a hall sink at the top of a dark tenement staircase, and "Midnight in Bottle Alley," which showed lodgers sleeping on the floor [*Figures 2.42 and 2.43*].[80] He also included images of the neighborhood's more picturesque aspects: the "Old Homestead" at 41 Mulberry Street; the neighborhood's sole mulberry tree; an altar in "Bandit's Roost" commemorating the feast of St. Rocco; and a stale-bread vendor, whose large braided breads Riis compared to "exaggerated crullers." In addition, Riis documented the locus of the Bend's most notorious recent crime: 55 Baxter Street, where Vincenzo Nino murdered "his hard-

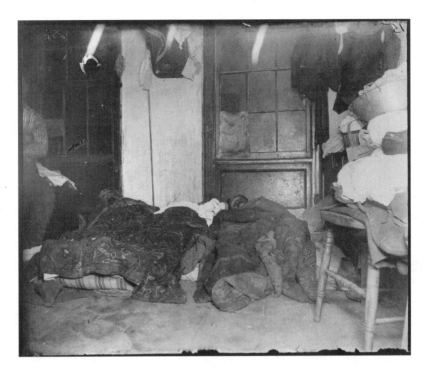

FIGURE 2.43 Jacob Riis, "Midnight in Bottle Alley," 1888–95, modern print from vintage negative, Jacob A. Riis Collection, MCNY, 90.13.4.161.

working, long-suffering wife." Instead of taking these picturesque views himself, Riis again turned to a professional photographer, this time an *Evening Sun* colleague named Collins.[81] Unlike many of Riis's photographs, Collins's more conventional images were taken from a considerable distance and did not require his interacting with his subjects. One photograph depicts Riis standing in front of a vegetable stand, but it was not used in the article [*Figure 2.44*].

FIGURE 2.44 [unknown] Collins, "A Vegetable Stand in the Mulberry Street Bend with Myself in the Picture," 1895, modern print from vintage negative, Jacob A. Riis Collection, MCNY, 90.13.4.270.

Riis wrote another article on "The Clearing of Mulberry Bend" for the *Review of Reviews*, a monthly magazine founded in 1891 and specializing in current events.[82] Most of its illustrations had appeared elsewhere, with the exception of Riis's only overview photograph of the Bend. The article also included photographs Riis had acquired from the Board of Health showing the nearby Five Points in 1872 before it was demolished, and the results of Colonel Waring's celebrated street cleaning program initiated in 1895.[83]

During the three-year administration of reform mayor William Strong, Riis temporarily set aside his skeptical attitude toward politics and shifted his efforts from public advocacy to government participation. In 1896, Teddy Roosevelt, who had admired *How the Other Half Lives*, was appointed president of the Police Board, and he and Riis, whose office was directly across from police headquarters on Mulberry Street, became friends. Against considerable protest, Roosevelt followed Riis's advice to close down the police lodging houses and set up a temporary shelter on an East River pier. A year later, the city opened a municipal lodging house at East 23rd Street and First Avenue. Modeled on the "Boston Plan," it offered decent beds, baths, and breakfast in exchange for a few hours' work. As agent of the Good Government Clubs, Riis advocated other reforms, which the Strong administration, sometimes reluctantly, also carried out: the establishment of a truant school, the demolition of the old Tombs, the abolition of cruller bakeries in tenements, and the allocation of funds for new schools in immigrant neighborhoods. Riis also identified the worst tenements for

FIGURE 2.45 Jacob Riis, "Old Barney in Cat Alley," 1898, modern print from vintage negative, Jacob A. Riis Collection, MCNY,
90.13.4.297.

demolition, including the infamous Gotham Court and Mott Street
Barracks. As secretary of the Citizens' Committee for Small Parks,
he chose the sites to be cleared for two East Side parks, which,
unlike Mulberry Bend Park, included playgrounds for children.

This torrent of activity left Riis little time for journalism and
even less for photography. In December 1895, Riis took seven

IN SLEEPING QUARTERS—RIVINGTON STREET DUMP.

FIGURE 2.46 "Real Wharf Rats," *Evening Sun*, March 18, 1892, Jacob A. Riis Papers, Library of Congress. Most newspapers reproduced Riis's photographs as single-line wood engravings, in which tone and detail were lost.

photographs of tenement residents, which he uncharacteristically identified by location and date,[84] and in 1896 he photographed the remnants of an unidentified shantytown. In 1897, he photographed the Old Marble Cemetery off Second Avenue for an *Evening Sun* article on the conversion of the cemetery into a playground, and in 1898 he photographed the sites cleared on Division Street and Bone Alley near Willetts Street for small parks.[85] Riis's last photographs were for a December 1898 *Century* article, "The Passing of

MULBERRY BEND.

THE CLEARING OF MULBERRY BEND.

THE STORY OF THE RISE AND FALL OF A TYPICAL NEW YORK SLUM.

BY JACOB A. RIIS.

IT is altogether appropriate that the going of the wickedest of American slums and the coming at last of a practical proposition for housing the poor decently in city tenements, and so of effectually outlawing slums hereafter, should occur simultaneously. Within a week I have seen such a plan, worked out by two enthusiastic girl architects, that promises to render life in a 25-foot tenement—the great stumbling block heretofore—not only tolerable, but even desirable to a degree, and have watched the tearing down of the rookeries in the Mulberry Bend to make room for a park. It seemed little less than a revolution to see them go down, looking back over the long struggle that had been so full of discouragement. In fact, it was just that. It marked the triumph of conscience and common sense over the selfishness and shortsighted greed, the dawn of a better and brighter day in municipal government which must henceforth be the government of the masses here as elsewhere; and in the retrospect the old slum was invested with a dignity impossible while it yet lived and had power for mischief: that of having served a useful purpose after all. The lesson it read us American cities may not for their own safety soon forget. For not only was the Mulberry Bend typical in many ways of city slums everywhere; it had a history. It was the whole story of the degradation of poverty by irresponsible wealth, of the criminal heedlessness of a day that took no thought for the morrow and piled up a fearful interest against its account, of absentee landlordism, of crime and squalor and suffering that will yet bear their evil fruit in generations to come, of " skin " building that never stopped to weigh human life in the scale against the dishonest dollar,

FIGURE 2.47 Jacob Riis, "The Clearing of Mulberry Bend," *Review of Reviews*, August 1895, 172, Jacob A. Riis Papers, Library of Congress. By 1895 halftones in weeklies and monthlies were common.

Cat Alley," which described the demolition of "my alley" across from his newspaper office in preparation for the widening of Elm Street.[86] The article was nostalgic, reflecting on the neighborhood's changes over twenty years, and telling the story of "Old Barney," a Civil War veteran and ex-locksmith who was its last inhabitant. Riis made a portrait of Barney clutching his enormous hoop of old keys and photographed the demolition crews at work [*Figure 2.45*].

When Riis published *How the Other Half Lives* in 1890, the half-tone reproduction was an experimental technology that had little effect on the publishing industry. By 1895, however, the process was commercially viable, and within two years' time it was standard practice. This development directly affected the appearance of Riis's photographs in print. Before 1895, daily newspapers hurriedly produced single-line wood engravings from Riis's photographs, which sacrificed detail and tonal gradation for crude, graphic clarity. For example, in the illustrations for "Real Wharf Rats" (1892), the dirt covering every person and object is completely lost in the single-line engravings, and the article does not indicate that the images were based on photographs [*Figure 2.46*]. By comparison, in "Where Santa Claus Will Not Go" (1895), the editor touted the article's halftone illustrations, noting that each one was "from a photograph taken especially for the *Journal*."[87]

The development of the halftone fueled the growth of the ten-cent monthly magazine, which by the mid-1890s challenged the dominance of the more expensive "quality" magazines. Typical of the new magazines was the *Review of Reviews*, which introduced

FIGURE 2.48 Jacob Riis, "Bringing in the Apple Crop," 1894, modern print from vintage negative, Jacob A. Riis Collection, MCNY, 90.13.4.216.

Riis's article "The Clearing of Mulberry Bend" with a large, half-page halftone of the author's photograph of the Bend [*Figure 2.47*]. Not all the new magazines, however, embraced the halftone. *Century Magazine*, which was acclaimed for its high-quality wood engravings, resisted halftones in favor of the artist's touch. In the 1895 article "One Way Out," for example, the illustrator Orson Lowell altered the compositions of Riis's photographs by adding

DRAWN BY ORSON LOWELL.   FROM A PHOTOGRAPH BY THE AUTHOR.
BRINGING IN THE APPLE CROP.

FIGURE 2.49 Orson Lowell, "Bringing in the Apple Crop," *Century Magazine*, December 1895, 304. Lowell added figures to the foreground of Riis's photograph. Compare with figure 2.48.

large, picturesque figures in the foreground [*Figures 2.48 and 2.49*]. Even after it substituted halftone reproductions for engravings, *Century* persisted in employing illustrators. In the 1898 "The Passing of Cat Alley," Jay Hambridge reworked Riis's photographs before they were reproduced as halftones, and the magazine credited Hambridge, not Riis, for the illustrations.

Riis could not predict or control the publishing process, nor did he seem to care. In his scrapbook, he meticulously corrected textual errors but did not mention the manner in which photographs were reworked or reproduced. In "Where Santa Claus Will Not Go," he corrected two captions that the *Journal* had invented. Crossing out the caption "Mother and Daughter," Riis wrote, "Lie. They are two spinster sisters." Correcting "Husband and Father in Jail," the caption for a photograph of a Ludlow Street family living in a cellar, he noted, "Rot. The husband is an honest butcher."[88] Sacrifice of tonal gradation or the addition of figures to his compositions invoked no similar protestations.

Although Riis was unconcerned with the mechanics and aesthetics of halftone illustration, the new technology and the growing appreciation of the publicity value of photographs directly affected him. To attract a wider audience, philanthropic and government agencies began enlisting professional photographers to document their activities. Beginning in 1894, for example, the Children's Aid Society used photographs in its annual reports, and in 1897 the Mayor's Committee for New York City illustrated its report on *Public Baths and Public Comfort Stations* with photographs by Emil Stopft, who made lantern slides on the same subject.[89] At the same time, the Byron Company, one of New York's most successful commercial firms, was hired to produce a series of photographs of tenement life.[90] The growing supply of such photographs eliminated the need for Riis to use his own camera, and after 1898 he never again took photographs to illustrate his writings.

Riis's Later Career: From Producing to Consuming Photographs

As the turn of the century approached, Riis's life changed direction, leading him farther away from the East Side and photography. In 1898, when Tammany regained control of City Hall, Riis's direct influence on citywide reform came to an abrupt halt, although he maintained some influence through Roosevelt, who was elected governor the next year. In 1899, after twenty-three years of newspaper reporting, Riis resigned his staff position at the *Evening Sun*, no longer needing its steady salary or enjoying its demanding routine. His frequent magazine bylines had enhanced his national reputation and increased the demand for his lectures, for which (with the assistance of professional booking agents) he earned as much as $150 a talk. Despite a heart attack in 1900, Riis began frenetically traveling the country, delivering as many as seventy lectures in a ninety-day period.

The publication of *The Making of an American* in 1901, the same year that Roosevelt became president, made Riis and his wife Elisabeth national celebrities. The story of a young immigrant's struggle to win the hand of his childhood sweetheart was an instant commercial success. That same year, the King's Daughters Settlement moved into spacious quarters at 48–50 Henry Street and renamed itself the Jacob A. Riis Settlement House. Deeply honored, Riis took responsibility for the settlement's mortgage, which he financed through his lecture fees. In 1903, Riis wrote a series of articles in *Outlook* about his relationship with Roosevelt, which was rushed to press as an adulatory campaign "biography." And he published *Children of the Tenements*, a compilation of stories that "came to me in the course of my work as police reporter for nearly a quarter of a century."[91] Although he kept his Mulberry Street office, Riis retreated during summers to a small cottage behind his house in Richmond Hill, where he concentrated on his writing. He was busier, wealthier, and more famous than ever before but increasingly removed from new developments in reform circles and from the life of the slums. His writings drew more heavily on memories than on fresh observation.

Riis's retrospective posture began in 1898, immediately after the defeat of Mayor William Strong. His new lecture on the "battle with the slum" formed the basis of a book, *The Ten Years' War: An Account of the Battle with the Slum in New York*, which Houghton Mifflin and Company published in 1900. Inscribed "to the faint-hearted and those of little faith," Riis preached optimism in the face of defeat. He looked back over the past decade, praising the achievements of the Strong administration, extolling the new settlement houses for spearheading "reform by humane touch," and detailing the accomplishments of the private sector, especially the Mills Hotels for homeless men and the model tenements of the City and Suburban Homes and Company. He also offered a sympathetic defense of recent immigrants, noting that he "ha[d] not the heart to shut anybody out."[92]

Beginning with a photograph of Sanitary Commissioner George E. Waring and ending with one of Police Commissioner Theodore Roosevelt, *The Ten Years' War* was sparsely illustrated. There were ten other photographs, only one of which was by Riis—an image of the Church Street police lodging house, which illustrated the story of his own homelessness. The remaining nine, including images of a model tenement, Mills House No. 1, Mulberry Bend Park, a new public school, a roof playground, and a newly paved street, were borrowed from the agencies responsible for those civic improvements. All of the photographs were reproduced as full-page half-tones, which by 1900 had become standard practice.

Although Riis's book was respectfully and warmly received, the real news in reform circles was the 1900 Tenement House Exhibition, organized by the Tenement House Committee of the Charity Organization Society (COS).[93] More than ten thousand people visited the two-week exhibition, which consisted of more than one hundred maps, six models, numerous statistical charts, plans, and drawings, and more than a thousand photographs. It was the handiwork of COS President Robert W. DeForest, a prominent New York City lawyer, and Lawrence Veiller, a young housing expert and former settlement house worker. Unlike earlier tenement house committees (those of 1879, 1884, and 1894), the new committee did not consider itself an investigative body or aim at specialists. As Riis explained, the exhibition was "the first attempt that has been made to gather up all the results of forty years' battle with the slum, and present them in [so comprehensive] a way."[94] In response, Governor Roosevelt established a Tenement House Commission, the work of which led to the passage of reform legislation in 1901 and to the establishment of a municipal Tenement House Department led by DeForest and Veiller.

Riis was not a member of the Tenement House Committee, but his enthusiastic support for its mission was understandable. DeForest and Josephine Shaw Lowell, COS's founder, were among his most trusted colleagues, and the goals of the 1900 exhibition and of Riis's book were essentially the same: to place tenement house reform in historical perspective and push forward its cause. Riis promoted the exhibition in a *Harper's Weekly* article and described the commission in a laudatory essay in the *Review of Reviews*.[95]

In addition to publicizing the exhibition, Riis lent several photographs to it. Among eighteen extant exhibition panels are three that include Riis's photographs from *How the Other Half Lives*.[96] "Gotham Court" appears in a panel illustrating "Notorious Tenements Now Destroyed," and "Five Cents a Spot" and "In Poverty Gap: An English Coal Heaver's Home" appear in panels illustrating the evils of the narrow airshafts between buildings, a product of the so-called dumbbell plan instituted in 1879. In his *Harper's* article, Riis explained the failure of these airshafts: "Twenty years' experience has shown the air-shaft to be largely a delusion and a snare, . . . [fostering] foul smells instead of fresh air

FIGURE 2.50 Unknown photographer, "Bathtub in an Airshaft," modern print from vintage copy negative, Jacob A. Riis Collection, MCNY, 90.13.4.49. Riis probably acquired this photograph from the 1900 Tenement House Exhibition Committee.

and, like a giant flue, spreading fires at deadly speed." Among the successes of the 1901 legislation was outlawing this design.

Notably, Riis took more photographs from the Tenement House Exhibition than he gave to it. He acquired photographs of architectural models and maps, clearings for new parks, model tenements, tenement backyards, and airshafts, all for use in his newly expanded lecture schedule.[97] During the same period, Riis obtained photographs from other sources as well: images of new school buildings, roof playgrounds, and vacation schools from the Board of Education; photographs of drawings of infamous tenements from the 1884 annual report of the New York Association for Improving the Condition of the Poor; portraits of many of his friends in the reform movement, including DeForest, Lowell, and Richard Watson Gilder; and a supply of anecdotal scenes, including humorous studies of children at play in a West 68th Street playground.

Riis gave these prints to a commercial photographer who tacked them to a board, photographed them (the thumbtacks are visible in the copies), and made lantern slides for lectures and copy prints for articles [*Figure 2.50*].[98] Once Riis had obtained the copy negatives, he had little use for the original prints, and many have disappeared. The addition of so many prints, lantern slides, and copy negatives convinced Riis to organize his collection. He placed each negative in an envelope, to which he affixed a number and a brief description of the image. And he compiled an inventory of the negatives in a pocket-sized notebook.[99] The inventory did not distinguish between original negatives and copies, since Riis valued them equally.

In 1902, the Macmillan Company published a new version of *The Ten Years' War*, entitled *The Battle with the Slum*, which included a preface in which Riis explained that "not in the thirty years before did we advance as in these three." The reference was not just to

FIGURE 2.51 Jacob Riis, "The Survival of the Unfittest," 1890–92, modern print from vintage negative, Jacob A. Riis Collection, MCNY, 90.13.4.205. Riis mentioned this photograph but did not reproduce it in *Children of the Poor* (1892).

the new Tenement House Department, but to the 1898 consolidation of Greater New York, which diminished Tammany's power; the 1901 election of Mayor Seth Low; and the commencement of construction for the new subway system, which would allow workers to live farther from Manhattan in less congested areas. *The Battle with the Slum* was a patchwork: three chapters of the earlier book were

FIGURE 2.52 Jacob Riis, "Tramps Lodging in a Jersey Street Yard," before 1898, modern print from vintage negative, Jacob A. Riis Collection, MCNY, 90.13.4.102. Jersey Street was demolished with the widening of Elm Street in 1898. Compare with "The Tramp," *Figure* 2.8 (page 141).

expanded to six chapters; four were repeated verbatim; chapters on Tammany and the public school building campaign were added; and three stories were borrowed from *Century Magazine.*

The biggest difference between *The Ten Years' War* and *The Battle with the Slum* was the increase in illustrations from twelve to ninety. Of that total, fourteen were from Riis's old negatives, eleven were from artists' drawings, and sixty-five were from newly acquired photographs. Organizing his collection had given Riis the opportunity to look anew at his old photographs, and the book included five that had never been published before.[100] The most interesting are two photographs taken by him in 1892—"The Survival of the Unfittest" and "Tramps Lodging in a Jersey Street Yard"—depicting backyards near his Mulberry Street office, when factories were replacing tenements [*Figures 2.51 and 2.52*].[101] The former shows a lone rear tenement surrounded by new commercial buildings, and the latter is of the location where Riis had encountered "The Tramp" in the winter of 1887 [*Figure 2.8*].[102]

In 1903, Riis was invited to give the first annual William L. Bull Lectures on Christian Sociology at the Philadelphia Divinity School. The lectures were published as *The Peril and the Preservation of the Home,* Riis's last book on poverty and reform. Two of the four lectures were slide presentations, and the book reproduced twenty- five of the photographs used in these lectures. Riis's themes were not new nor were the illustrations, which consisted primarily of photographs from *How the Other Half Lives, Children of the Poor,* and *The Battle with the Slum.* What was new was the copyright beneath each previously published photograph. By 1903 Scribner's and Macmillan had learned that Riis's photographs, as well as his words, were valuable property.

Although Riis never again published a book on reform, he did author a steady stream of articles on the subject. The illustrations for these articles were supplied by magazine editors, who found it increasingly easy to locate relevant images or hire photographers to work on assignment. For example, in 1905 and 1906, Riis wrote three articles for the *Christian Herald, An Illustrated Family Magazine* on the immigrants of the East Side, which were illustrated with photographs by unnamed professionals [*Figure 2.53*].[103] For articles published in 1907 and 1908 in *Garden Magazine,* the photographers were credited by name.[104] Riis, in turn, found these photographs useful for his lectures and began to acquire them. In a letter dated June 30, 1909, he asked the administrator of the Jacob A. Riis Settlement to help track down photographs of the settlement from a magazine photographer:

> Have you negatives or good photos of the two pictures in the garden magazine of December 1907. . . . If you have them, will you keep them for me—I want slides made of them. If not, will you send to the photographer who took them and ask him to make them. They are to be the usual size.[105]

In 1911, Riis again went in search of photographs, this time to illustrate his article "A Modern St. George: The Growth of

NEW YORK, SEPTEMBER 27, 1905

THE CHRISTIAN HERALD

AN ILLUSTRATED FAMILY MAGAZINE

THE HEART OF THE JEWISH QUARTER   AN EAST SIDE ITALIAN FAMILY   ON CROWDED LUDLOW STREET

The Golden Rule in Poverty Row

By JACOB A. RIIS

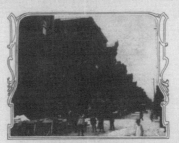

AMONG THE HESTER STREET TENEMENTS

CONTINUED ON PAGE 757

FIGURE 2.53 "The Golden Rule in Poverty Row," *Christian Herald*, September 27, 1905, Jacob A. Riis Papers, Library of Congress. These halftone illustrations were made from photographs by unidentified photographers.

Organized Charity in the United States," which appeared in the
October issue of *Scribner's Magazine*, the same journal that had
published his landmark essays "How the Other Half Lives" and
"Children of the Poor." Although historical in scope, the article
dealt extensively with recent innovations: Sea Breeze, a convales-
cent home for tubercular children on Coney Island; Caroline Rest,
a "school for mothers" in the Hudson Valley; and the Children's
Aid Society's farm school in Westchester County. The article also
discussed the efforts of the National Consumers League to regulate
hours and labor conditions for women and children.

Riis had little difficulty finding the photographs when he needed
them. In 1905, he was appointed to the publications committee of the COS, which produced the pioneer social work journal
Charities and the Commons. COS files and those of the Children's
Aid Society, both of which organizations were headquartered in
the Charities Building at Park Avenue and 22nd Street, provided
repositories of images. Among the National Consumers League
photographs that Riis acquired were two by Jessie Tarbox Beals, an
enterprising commercial photographer who worked extensively for
the COS from 1910 through the 1920s. From the National Child
Labor Committee (NCLC), Riis obtained thirteen photographs
by Lewis Hine, a young "social photographer," who in 1908 was
appointed staff photographer for *Charities and the Commons*, which
in 1909 was renamed the *Survey*. Riis responded strongly to Hine's
powerful images of children working in a Mississippi cotton mill, a
Virginia glass factory, and a Pennsylvania coal mine. Although their

A few of the boys who work on a night shift in a Virginia glass factory.

FIGURE 2.54 Lewis Hine, "A Modern Saint George," *Scribner's Magazine*, October 1911, 397. Riis acquired this and ten other Hine photographs from the National Child Labor Committee.

connection to his text was tenuous, Riis included seven Hine photographs in "A Modern St. George" [*Figure 2.54*].

In 1905, Elisabeth died suddenly of pneumonia, leaving Riis devastated. His two youngest children were still at home, and his three oldest required financial support. Two years later, he married his secretary, Mary Phillips, twenty-eight years his junior, who restored happiness and stability to his life. Despite deteriorating health, Riis continued to work feverishly. In 1912, they moved from New York City to Barre, Massachusetts, where Mary hoped to establish a profitable farm. There Riis died of a heart attack in 1914 at the age of sixty-five.

The Significance of Riis's Photography

This reconstruction confirms Riis's own account of his interest in photography: the discovery of flashlight photography launched his career; he took photographs himself for only a brief period, most actively from 1888 to 1892; and he was "a photographer after a fashion," not a serious amateur, let alone a professional. Riis developed his reform ideas in lectures in which photographs dominated his presentation, and then condensed and refined those themes into articles and books in which photographs were secondary to his texts. Indeed, photographs had no meaning for him independent of his narrative; they served only to enliven his stories and substantiate his arguments. All of this explains why Riis made no serious effort to preserve his photographic materials, leaving them in a box in an attic where they remained undisturbed for thirty years.

Riis never developed what John Szarkowski has called "a photographer's eye"—an aesthetic approach to composing photographs—although he did refine his use of the camera. His first photographs, which appeared in *How the Other Half Lives*, were indistinguishable from those he had commissioned from Lawrence and Piffard.

Some were staged vignettes that relied on stereotypes of the urban poor; some were composed in daylight with the cooperation of their subjects; and still others were taken indoors in near or total darkness, resulting in haphazardly composed scenes that function as metaphors for urban chaos and degradation. By contrast, many of Riis's photographs for *Children of the Poor* depend for their effectiveness on his having established rapport with his subjects, several of whom he interviewed extensively. This change toward more nuanced portraits paralleled a shift in Riis's writing away from the slum tour to colorful stories about individuals.

Riis's interest in taking photographs always remained tentative. Even when he was still using the camera, he hired professional photographers Fisk and Collins to do work for him. And after 1898, when his focus shifted toward chronicling the reforms of the past decade, he chose to collect photographs, not take them, and he more than doubled his collection by acquiring prints from a variety of sources and having them copied. In his later lectures and writings, Riis established the "problem" of urban poverty by repeatedly showing the same few disturbing images, such as "Five Cents a Spot" or "A Scrub and Her Bed," and he larded his publications with commercial photographs that contributed to his arguments but carried little visual interest.

How the Other Half Lives inspired imitators immediately. In 1892, *Darkness and Daylight, or, Lights and Shadows of New York Life* was published, which included 250 line engravings "from special photographs taken from life expressly for this work, mostly by

A SLY OPIUM SMOKER.

(This photograph was made by flash-light in a Chinese opium den on Pell street when the smoker was supposed to be fast asleep. Subsequently the photograph disclosed the fact that he had at least one eye open when the picture was made.)

FIGURE 2.55 "A Sly Opium Smoker," *Darkness and Daylight, or, Lights and Shadows of New York Life* (A.D. Worthington, 1892), 571. This wood engraving was made after Riis's "Chinese Opium Joint." Compare *Figure 2.7* (page 140).

flashlight." Most of the photographs were by Oscar G. Mason, a respected professional photographer on staff at Bellevue Hospital, but a dozen were by Riis, who was thanked in the publisher's preface [*Figure 2.55*].[106] That same year, an imitation of Riis's slide lecture was published by T.H. McAllister Optical Company of New York, one of the country's leading manufacturers of lantern slides.

FIGURE 2.56 "A Rookery in Mulberry Bend," *The Dark Side of New York* (T.H. McAllister Optical Company of New York, 1892), lantern slide. Collection of Tom Rall Flea Mark at Eastern Market, Arlington, Virginia. In this case, McAllister pirated one of Riis's images. Compare *Figure 2.11* (page 148).

Entitled *The Dark Side of New York*, it included "nearly 200 views illustrating the wretched conditio ns under which the lower 'other half' of our dense population live and die," and was offered for sale along with Riis's book [*Figure 2.56*].[107] In 1907, the Chicago

FIGURE 2.57 *The Shadows of a Great City — or — The Slums of New York* (Chicago Projecting Company, 1905), sales catalogue, 350, Collection of Jack Judson, 1419 Austin Highway, San Antonio, Texas, 78209.

Projecting Company offered a set of sixty slides of *The Shadows of a Great City—or—The Slums of New York* [*Figure 2.57*]. The accompanying lecture, however, departed from Riis's script, substituting an old-fashioned temperance lecture, which placed the blame for poverty on the individual rather than on the environment. The slide set included scenes that bore Riis's titles—"Street Arabs," "Growler Gang," and "Wharf Rats"—but were not his images, along with traditional temperance subjects, such as "The Drunkard's Widow" and "The Drunkard's Child in Prayer."[108]

Although *How the Other Half Lives* inspired imitators, Riis's photographs seem to have had little impact on the photographs of Progressive Era photographers. That may be attributed to the vagaries of the reproductive techniques of his time, which compromised the full impact of his most original work. In the early 1890s, Riis made photographs that no one had made before, but not until 1900 could the general public view them effectively in print. By then, his photographs were no longer original, and he was showcasing only a handful of them in his lectures and writings.

Although Riis has been described as "America's first true journalist-photographer,"[109] it was the Progressives, not Riis, who pioneered photojournalism. In the 1900 Tenement House Exhibition, organizer Lawrence Veiller used Riis's photographs in a manner that was as new to Riis as it was to the general public. Instead of presenting a small number of images in the context of a narrative, Veiller displayed masses of photographs, artfully arranged, with minimal text. In one of the extant exhibition panels, Riis's photograph

"Lodgers in a Tenement, Five Cents a Spot" is placed in the center, with photographs of airshafts taken by another photographer occupying the four corners [*Figure 2.58*]. Another panel displays Riis's photograph of an English coal heaver and his family and is similarly surrounded by four airshaft photographs [*Figure 2.59*]. Together, the panels show the two extremes of tenement life—the unruly lives of the lodgers and the orderly home of the coal heaver—both circumscribed by the claustrophobic walls of the airshaft. Veiller's innovative use of photographic display became the prototype for exhibitions from the turn of the century to the New Deal, elucidating a wide array of social problems from child labor practices to tuberculosis.

Riis's name is often linked with that of Lewis Hine, the leading practitioner of "social photography" in the Progressive Era, but there is little connection between the photographs of the two men. Riis collected Hine's photographs, and Hine may well have read Riis's books, but the heavily reworked halftones of *Children of the Poor* would have been inconsequential to him. It was Hine's "photo-stories" in the *Survey*, which presented narratives in series of captioned photographs, that were the direct precursors of the photo-essays of 1930s' illustrated magazines. Moreover, although Riis and Hine traveled in similar reform circles, they lived in different worlds. Riis believed that the modern city was a Christian fraternity in which each "half" could redeem "the other": helping the poor uplifted the rich, and adopting the norms of the Christian home uplifted the poor.[110] Hine subscribed to the Progressives' faith

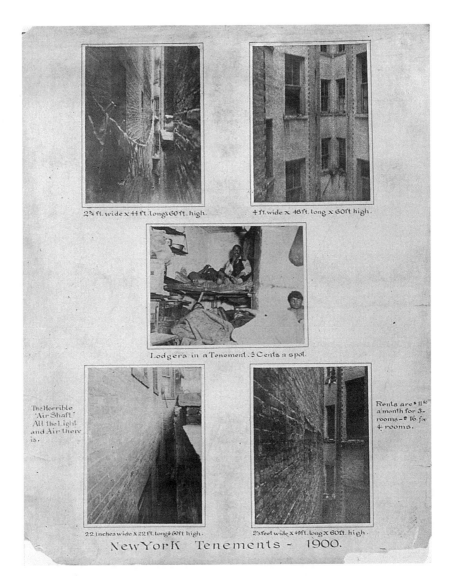

FIGURE 2.58 "New York Tenements, 1900," Tenement House
Committee exhibition panel, Museum of the City of New York.

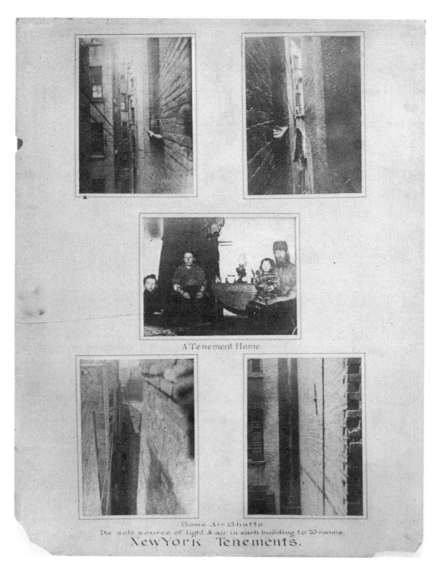

A Tenement Home.

Some Air Shafts.
The sole source of light & air in each building to 70 rooms.
NewYork Tenements.

FIGURE 2.59 "New York Tenements," Tenement House Committee exhibition panel, Museum of the City of New York.

in scientific expertise and the bureaucratic management of social problems. Hine was a trained sociologist, while Riis was fundamentally a preacher who delivered powerful and entertaining sermons supported by statistics and photographs.

One of Riis's final achievements captures the spirit of his distinctive approach to reform in the modern city. To celebrate Christmas in 1912, Riis arranged for a sixty-foot tree to be erected in Madison Square and lit it with 1,200 electric lights. On Christmas Eve, ten thousand people cheered as the New York Edison Company turned on the power to illuminate the tree. A week later, as an antidote to the growing rowdiness of New Year's Eve celebrations, Riis organized a musical program to take place around the tree, setting up stereopticons to project the words to the songs on huge screens. For this year-end celebration, a crowd of one hundred thousand people assembled, and as the clock on the Metropolitan Tower struck midnight they all sang "America." In a letter describing the event to his daughter, Riis dubbed himself "stage manager and musical director" and wrote: "I feel that I have given New York something that will last and be for the good to the farthest generation. We have broken the back of the ugly nightmare that has disgraced us too long."[111]

For Jacob Riis, photography, like the giant tree and electric lights, created a spectacle intended to grab the hearts of his audience.

Notes

Introduction

1. Our thanks to Kevin P. Murphy, who as a research assistant on this project shared with us his essay, "Useful Citizen: The Legacy of Jacob A. Riis," 2000.

2. Robert W. DeForest and Lawrence Veiller, *The Tenement House Problem* (New York: Macmillan, 1903), vol. 1, 105.

3. "Jacob Riis," *Outlook*, June 6, 1914, 284.

4. "Jacob Augustus Riis," *Dictionary of American Biography*, 1936. See also Frances Perkins, *The Reminiscences of Frances Perkins*, Columbia University, Oral History Collection, 6–7; and Thomas Kessner, *Fiorello H. La Guardia and the Making of Modern New York* (New York, 1989), 23–24.

5. *Jacob A. Riis: Police Reporter, Reformer, Useful Citizen* (New York: D. Appleton-Century Co. Inc., 1939).

6. "The Living Heritage of Jacob Riis," *New York Times Magazine*, May 1, 1949, 12–13ff.

7. Beaumont Newhall, *The History of Photography from 1839 to the Present Day* (Museum of Modern Art, 1949), 167–71.

8. Roy Lubove, ed., intro., *The Making of an American* (New York: Harper & Row, 1966); J. Riis Owre, preface and epilogue, *The Making of an American* (New York: Macmillan Company, 1970); Sam Bass Warner, Jr., ed., intro.,

How the Other Half Lives: Studies Among the Tenements of New York, The John Harvard Library (Cambridge, MA: Belknap Press of Harvard University Press, 1970); Charles A. Madison, preface, *How the Other Half Lives: Studies Among the Tenements of New York* (New York: Dover Publications, 1971); Francesco Cordasco, intro., *Children of the Poor* (New York: Garrett Press, 1970); Francesco Cordasco, ed., intro., *Jacob Riis Revisited: Poverty and the Slum in Another Era* (Garden City, NY: Anchor Books, 1968); James B. Lane, *Jacob A. Riis and the American City* (Port Washington, NY: Kennikat Press, 1974); Edith Patterson Meyer, *"Not Charity, but Justice": The Story of Jacob A. Riis*, (New York: Vanguard Press, 1974); Alexander Alland, Sr., *Jacob A. Riis: Photographer and Citizen* (Millerton, NY: Aperture Foundation, 1974).

9. Cordasco, *Jacob Riis Revisited*, xxii.

10. See, for example, Sally Stein, "Making Connections with the Camera: Photography and Social Mobility in the Career of Jacob Riis," *Afterimage*, May 1983, pp. 9–16, and Keith Gandal, *The Virtues of the Vicious: Jacob Riis, Stephen Crane, and the Spectacle of the Slum* (New York: Oxford University Press, 1997).

11. United Nations Human Settlements Programme, *The Challenge of Slums: Global Report on Human Settlement* (London and Sterling, VA: Earthscan, 2003). See also Mike Davis, *Planet of Slums* (London and New York: Verso, 2006).

1. Jacob Riis's New York

1. Theodore Roosevelt, *An Autobiography* (New York and London, 1913), 70. The most comprehensive biography of Riis is James B. Lane, *Jacob A. Riis and the American City* (Port Washington, NY, 1974), which has superseded Louise Ware, *Jacob A. Riis: Police Reporter, Reformer, and Useful Citizen* (New York, 1939). See also David Leviatin, "Framing the Poor: The Irresistibility of How the Other Half Lives," an introductory essay to the recent Bedford/St. Martin's edition of *How the Other Half Lives* (Boston and New York, 1996),

1–50. All these works are heavily reliant upon Riis's own autobiography, *The Making of an American* (New York, 1903).

2. Entry for New Year's Eve, 1871, Jacob A. Riis, Diary, 1871–1875, trans. Lone Thygesen Blecher, in Jacob A. Riis Papers, New York Public Library, 38–39. Hereafter cited as Riis Diary.

3. Riis Diary, January 12, 1872, 52–53.

4. Riis Diary, Christmas Day, 1871, 30–31; March 5, 1872, 57–58.

5. Riis Diary, August 15, 1872, 107–8. See also entries for September 8, 15, and October 17, 1872.

6. Riis Diary, June 14, 1874, 68.

7. Riis, *Making of an American*, 184.

8. Riis, *Making of an American*, 135, 228, 202. For Riis's memories of his early newspaper days, see 126–51; 200–23.

9. Riis, *Making of an American*, 203–4. On the nature of late-nineteenth-century policing and the subsequent decline of police welfare work, see Erik H. Monkkonen, *Police in Urban America, 1860–1920* (Cambridge, 1981), 1–29, 86–128; Christopher P. Thale, "Civilizing New York City: Police Patrol, 1880–1935" (PhD dissertation, University of Chicago, 1995), esp. 342–71; James Lardwer and Thomas Reppetto, *NYPD: A City and Its Police* (New York, 2000), 50–71.

10. "People Who Disappear," *New York World*, June 4, 1883; "Secrets of the River," *New York World*, May 25, 1883. These clippings are in a collection of newspaper articles written by Riis, 1881–1892, container 12, Jacob A. Riis Papers, Library of Congress. Hereafter cited as Riis Clippings, LC.

11. "The Era of Suicides," *New York Mail & Express*, October 9, 1884; "The Foundling Boom," *New York Morning Journal*, April 15, 1883, Riis Clippings, LC.

12. "Removing the Dead," *New York Morning Journal*, April 4, 1883; "The Army of Cranks," *New York Morning Journal*, March 20, 1883; "Men with Pistols," *New York Mercury*, August 26, 1883; "Searching Prisoners," *New York World*, June 18, 1883, Riis Clippings, LC.

13. "1400 Years in Jail," *New York Morning Journal*, April 15, 1883; "The

Rogues Gallery" and "Chamber of Horrors," *New York Morning Journal,* April 21, 1883. See also "Police Conundrums," *Sunday Mercury,* March 23, 1884, and "Art in Banco Steering," *New York World,* April 6, 1884, Riis Clippings, LC. For background on Byrnes, see Daniel Czitrom, " 'Our Police Protectors': Authority and Corruption in Turn of the Century New York," paper delivered at the Organization of American Historians, Chicago, March 29, 1996.

14. "The Oldest 'Finest,' " *New York Morning Journal,* April 29, 1883. See also "Talent on the Force," *New York Morning Journal,* June 19, 1888, and "The Riot Relief Fund: Money for Brave Policemen" *New York Mail and Express,* January 1887, Riis Clippings, LC.

15. "The Ambulance Service," *New York World,* August 1883, Riis Clippings LC. On the centrality and historical contingency of racial categories and racial difference in Riis's era, two books in particular have informed my thinking: Matthew Frye Jacobson, *Whiteness of a Different Color: European Immigrants and the Alchemy of Race* (Cambridge, 1998), and Thomas G. Dyer, *Theodore Roosevelt and the Idea of Race* (Baton Rouge, 1980). See also the old but still insightful work by Richard Hofstadter, *Social Darwinism in American Thought,* rev. ed. (New York, 1959).

16. "Gotham Doings," *Green Bay Advance,* March 14, 1884; [Jacob Riis], "A Silver Deposit in Mott Street," *New York Tribune,* November 7, 1884, 8, Riis Clippings, LC.

17. "Pestilence in Nurseries. Summer Sufferings of Dwellers in Tenement Houses," *New York World,* June 11, 1883. See also "Epidemic Dangers," *New York Morning Journal,* April 17, 1883, Riis Clippings, LC. Statistics are from the Board of Health, as reported by Riis.

18. John H. Griscom, *The Sanitary Condition of the Laboring Population of New York* (New York, 1845), 5, 23, 48. On Griscom's importance and influence, see also John Duffy, *A History of Public Health in New York City, 1625–1866* (New York, 1968), 302–15; Elizabeth Blackmar, *Manhattan for Rent, 1785–1850* (Ithaca, 1989), 262–64; James Ford, *Slums and Housing, with Special Reference to New York City* (Cambridge, MA, 1936), 102–10;

Richard Plunz, A *History of Housing in New York City: Dwelling Type and Social Change in the American Metropolis* (New York, 1990), 4–7.

19. Charles E. Rosenberg (with Carroll S. Rosenberg), "Piety and Social Action: Some Origins of the American Public Health Movement," in *No Other Gods: On Science and American Social Thought* (Baltimore, 1976), 110; Griscom, *Sanitary Condition*, 3, 23, 12.

20. Robert Hartley, "Address to the Advisory Committee and Visitors," March 3, 1847, quoted in Lillian Brandt, *Growth and Development of AICP and COS* (New York, 1942), 19–20 (emphasis in original). For more background on the AICP, see Dorothy G. Becker, "The Visitor to the New York City Poor, 1843–1920" (DSW thesis, Columbia University, 1960), 3–133; Christine Stansell, *City of Women: Sex and Class in New York, 1789–1860* (New York, 1986), 202–15; Rosenberg, "Piety and Social Action."

21. NYAICP, *First Report of a Committee on the Sanitary Condition of the Poor in the City of New York* (New York, 1853). On the "Big Flat," see Robert H. Bremner, "The Big Flat: History of a New York Tenement House," *American Historical Review* 64 (October 1958): 54–62. On Gotham Court, see Ford, *Slums and Housing*, 166–68; 877–78; Plunz, *History of Housing in NYC*, 6–8; "Gotham Court," *Frank Leslie's Sunday Magazine*, June 1879, 655.

22. New York State Assembly, *Report of the Select Committee Appointed to Examine into the Condition of Tenant Houses in New York and Brooklyn*, Assembly Document No. 205, March 9, 1857, 3, 39, 51–52. For a somewhat different interpretation of this report see Stansell, *City of Women*, 200–202. See also Duffy, *History of Public Health*, 528–30.

23. [Stephen Smith], "Riots and Their Prevention," *American Medical Times* 7 (July 25, 1863): 41–42.

24. Citizens' Association, *Report of the Council of Hygiene and Public Health of the Citizens' Association of New York Upon the Sanitary Condition of the City* (New York, 1865), xv.

25. Citizens' Association, *Report*, lxviii, 64–65.

26. Janes quoted in Citizens' Association, *Report*, 249; Smith quote is from his manuscript notebook for Sanitary Inspection District 9, Seventh Ward, 88,

in *Sanitary Inspections*, New York City, 9 vols., New-York Historical Society, the only surviving fragments of the manuscript notebooks for the project.

On popular doubts about scientific thinking and the medical profession in these years, see Charles E. Rosenberg, *The Cholera Years* (Chicago, 1962), 208–12; Sandra Opdycke, *No One Was Turned Away: The Role of Public Hospitals in New York City Since 1900* (New York, 1999); David Rosner, *A Once Charitable Enterprise: Hospitals and Health Care in Brooklyn and New York, 1885–1915* (New York, 1982).

27. On the creation of the Metropolitan Board of Health, see Stephen Smith, *The City That Was* (New York, 1911); Gert H. Brieger, "Sanitary Reform in New York City: Stephen Smith and the Passage of the Metropolitan Health Bill," *Bulletin of the History of Medicine* 40 (September–October 1966): 407–29; Rosenberg, *The Cholera Years*, 175–212; Duffy, *History of Public Health*, 540–70; Lubove, *Progressives and the Slums*, 20–28; Edward B. Dalton, "The Metropolitan Board of Health," *North American Review* 106 (April 1868): 351–75. On the Tenement House Law of 1867, see Robert W. DeForest and Lawrence Veiller, *The Tenement House Problem* (New York, 1903), vol. 1, 94–97; Lubove, *Progressives and the Slums*, 25–28; Ford, *Slums and Housing*, 140–55; Plunz, *History of Housing in NYC*, 21–23.

28. Charles F. Chandler, "Address Before New York County Medical Society, June 3, 1878" (stenographer's minutes); Real Estate Owners' and Tax-payers' Association of the City of New York, "Memorial of Tenement House Owners, 1875–76, To the Legislature of the State of New York," both in Charles F. Chandler Papers, Rare Book and Manuscript Library, box 14, Columbia University.

29. Henry C. Meyer, *The Story of the Sanitary Engineer, Later the Engineering Record* (New York, 1928), 2; "Introduction," *Plumber and Sanitary Engineer* 1 (December 1877): 1. Hereafter cited as *Sanitary Engineer*. For background on the emerging profession of sanitary engineering, see Stanley K. Schultz and Clay McShane, "To Engineer the Metropolis: Sewers, Sanitation, and City Planning in Late Nineteenth Century America," *Journal of American History* 65 (September 1978): 389–411.

30. DeForest and Veiller, *Tenement House Problem*, 101–102. On the Tenement House Act of 1879, see Plunz, *History of Housing in NYC*, 24–27; Lubove, *Progressives and the Slums*, 28–32; "The Tenement House Problem," *Thirty Sixth Annual Report of the New York Association for Improving the Condition of the Poor* (New York, 1879), 37–55.

31. "The Main Source of Crime," *New York Times*, February 24, 1879, 5; "Improved Tenement Houses," *New York Tribune*, March 12, 1879, 2; "Our Bad Tenement Houses," *New York Times*, March 1, 1879, 8. For a different, and more lurid, account of Godwin's remarks, see "Tenement Life in New York," *Harper's Weekly*, March 22, 1879, 226.

32. "Our Bad Tenement Houses," *New York Times*, March 12, 1879, 2, and "Improved Tenement Houses," *New York Tribune*, March 12, 1879, 2.

33. Jared Day, *Urban Castles: Tenement Housing and Landlord Activism in New York City, 1890–1943* (New York, 1999), 54–55. Day's first two chapters offer an excellent analysis of the legal and economic aspects of the tenement business.

34. Chandler quoted in "Principles of Sanitary Science," *New York Tribune*, February 28, 1879, 5. On Chandler's work as Board of Health president, see also Duffy, *History of Public Health*, 55–77, and Chandler Papers, boxes 14–16.

35. Meyer, *Story of the Sanitary Engineer*, 48. For contemporary accounts of Chandler's use of magic-lantern slides, see ibid., and "The Public Health," *New York Times*, November 26, 1879, 2; "The Health of New York," *New York Daily Tribune*, November 26, 1879, 1; "Editor's Table," *The Sanitarian* 7 (April 1879): 177–81.

36. James D. McCabe Jr., *Lights and Shadows of New York Life* (Philadelphia, 1872), 696–97. See tenement house illustrations on 684 and 688. For an overview of this literature, see Daniel Czitrom, "The Secrets of the Great City," in Ric Burns and James Sanders, *New York: An Illustrated History* (New York, 1999), 210–15.

37. Edward Crapsey, "Tenement Life," in *The Nether Side of New York* (New York, 1872), 113, 116.

38. Stephen Smith, *The City That Was* (New York, 1911; reprinted. Metuchen NJ, 1973), 89–90. For examples of illustrations in the *Sanitary Engineer,* see "Homes of the Poor," November 1878, 262–63 (contrasting model tenements with existing ones), and "Inner Life of the Poor," December 1878, 11 (reproducing images from the Citizens Association 1865 report. For examples of illustrated articles, see "Our Homeless Poor; or 'How the Other Half of the World Lives,' " *Frank Leslie's Illustrated Newspaper;* March 9, 1872, 407ff; "A City Tenement House," *Harper's Weekly* 17; September 13, 1873, 796; John W. Cramer, "The Story of a Tenement House," *Frank Leslie's Sunday Magazine;* June 1879, 641–52.

39. "Tenement Life in New York," and "Black Holes in New York," *Harper's Weekly* 23, March 22, 1879, 226, 223.

40. See the following *Harper's Weekly* illustrations: William A. Rogers, "Tenement Life in New York—Sketches in 'Bottle Alley,' " March 22, 1879, 224; Charles Graham, "Tenement Life in New York—Sketches in the Fourth Ward," March 29, 1879, 245; William A. Rogers, "Tenement Life in New York—Rag-Pickers' Court, Mulberry Street," April 5, 1879, 265; Sol Eytinge Jr., "Among the Tenement Houses During the Heated Term—Just Before Daybreak," August 9, 1879, 629; C.A. Keetles, "A Beer Saloon in Bottle Alley," February 28, 1880, 140. For comparisons to Riis, see the following photos and line drawings from the original version of *How the Other Half Lives:* "Gotham Court" (frontispiece); "At the Cradle of the Tenement" (30); "Bottle Alley" (66); "Five Cents a Spot" (69). The best in-depth analysis of pictorial journalism in this era is Joshua Brown, *Beyond the Lines: Pictorial Reporting, Everyday Life, and the Crisis of Gilded Age America* (Berkeley, 2002).

41. "Tenement Life in New York," *Harper's Weekly*, March 22, 1879, 226, 227; and March 29, 1879, 246.

42. *Forty-first Annual Report of the New York Association for Improving the Condition of the Poor* (New York, 1884), 35, 36, 43, 53–54.

43. Moses Rischin, *The Promised City: New York's Jews, 1870–1914* (Cambridge, 1962), 201; Riis, *Making of an American,* 247. See also Riis, *Battle with the Slum,* 71–72. For background on Adler, see Horace L. Friess,

Felix Adler and Ethical Culture (New York, 1981), esp. 16–106, and Howard B. Radest, *Felix Adler: An Ethical Culture* (New York, 1998).

44. Quotes are from the following articles, written by Jacob Riis for the *New York Tribune*, covering Adler's lectures: "The Tenement House Question," February 4, 1884, 3; "Room for a Great Agitation," February 18, 1884, 3; "Tenement House Reform," March 3, 1884, 2.

45. Adler quoted in "The Miseries of Poverty," *New York Times*, December 15, 1884, 8. For examples of Riis's reporting on the commission see the following stories in the *New York Tribune*: "Tenement House Reform," October 15, 1884, 10; "Reforming Tenement Houses," December 15, 1884, 3; "Downtown Rookeries Condemned," December 18, 1884, 8; "Evils in Tenement Houses," February 18, 1885, 2.

46. Adler quoted in "Miseries of Poverty," *New York Times*, December 15, 1884, 3. See also Riis's account in "Reforming Tenement Houses," *New York Tribune*, December 15, 1884, 3. For background on Hill and her work in London, see Ellen Chase, *Tenant Friends in Old Deptford* (London, 1929).

47. [Jacob Riis], "Tenement House Reform," *New York Daily Tribune*, March 10, 1884, 8. In 1885 Adler helped organize the Tenement House Building Company; it built six model buildings on Cherry Street costing $155,000, but without any government subsidy. See [Jacob Riis], "Reforming Tenement Houses," *New York Tribune*, December 15, 1884, 3; "The Miseries of Poverty," *New York Times*, December 15, 1884, 8; Rischin, *Promised City*, 202.

48. "The Miseries of Poverty," *New York Times*, December 15, 1884, 8; "Reforming Tenement Houses," *New York Tribune*, 3.

49. New York State Senate, *Report of Tenement House Commission*, Senate Documents, vol. 5, no. 36, 1885, 31, 33–34.

50. Roosevelt, *Autobiography*, p. 89; New York (State), Court of Appeals, *In the Matter of the Application of Peter Jacobs*, 98 N.Y. 98 (1885), 105, 110, 115. In *How the Other Half Lives*, Riis discussed the *Jacobs* case in the chapter "The Bohemians—Tenement Cigar Making," 136–47. For the best recent overview of the *Jacobs* case, with special attention to its complex gender, class,

and ethnic dimensions, see Eileen Boris, " 'A Man's Dwelling House Is His Castle': Tenement House Cigarmaking and the Judicial Imperative," in *Work Engendered: Toward a New History of American Labor,* ed. Ava Baron (Ithaca, 1991), 114–41. See also Patricia A. Cooper, *Once a Cigar Maker: Men, Women, and Work Culture in American Cigar Factories, 1900–1919* (Urbana, 1987), 20–26; Samuel Gompers, *Seventy Years of Life and Labor: An Autobiography* (New York, 1925), 183–98. "The CMIU Campaign Against Tenement House Cigar Manufacture in New York City," in *The Samuel Gompers Papers,* vol. 1, ed. Stuart B. Kaufman (Urbana, 1986), 169–210, offers a valuable range of primary source documents on the campaign.

51. Meyer, *Story of the Sanitary Engineer,* 8. Biographical data on Wingate from *Appleton's Cyclopedia of American Biography* (New York, 1889), 564, and *Who Was Who in America,* vol. 1, 1897–1942 (Chicago, 1942), 1,365. For Wingate's early writings, see his series "An Episode in Municipal Government," *North American Review* 119 (October 1874): 359–408; 120 (January 1875): 119–55; 121 (July 1875): 113–55; 123 (October 1876): 362–425; *Views and Interviews on Journalism* (New York, 1875). On his work as a sanitary engineer, see, for example, "Foul Air in Houses," *New York Times,* February 3, 1882, 2; "The Unsanitary Homes of the Rich," *North American Review* 137 (August 1883): 172–84; "Practical Hints About Tenement Sanitation," *Lend a Hand* 2 (February 1887): 82–83.

52. The nine articles by Wingate, published weekly in the *New York Tribune:* "The Cradle of Cholera: Italian Dives and Dens," November 30, 1884, 4; "The Cradle of Cholera: Life in the Hebrew Quarter," December 7, 1884, 13; "In the Shadow of Trinity: Rookeries of the First Ward," December 14, 1884, 6; "Under the Great Bridge: Slums of the Fourth Ward," December 21, 1884 6; "Tenement House Problem: The Facts Broadly Stated," December 28, 1884, 4; "Overcrowded Tenements," January 4, 1885, 10; "Effects of Tenement Life," January 11, 1885, 10; "Causes of Overcrowding," February 1, 1885, 4; "The Tenement Problem," February 22, 1885, 4.

53. "The Cradle of Cholera: Italian Dives and Dens." In an editorial, the *Tribune* praised Wingate effusively: "The guide is discreet, wasting no time in

moralizing, but passing rapidly from house to house and from basement to garret, allowing the interiors to speak for themselves and to explain the hard realities of poverty in a great city" ("A Walk About Old Trinity," December 14, 1884, 8).

54. *Report of Tenement House Commission*, 45. See also table L, Tenant Statistics, 70–73.

55. "The Cradle of Cholera: Life in the Hebrew Quarter."

56. "In the Shadow of Trinity: Rookeries of the First Ward"; "Under the Great Bridge: The Slums of the Fourth Ward."

57. Charles F. Wingate, "The Moral Side of the Tenement House Problem," *Catholic World* 41 (May 1885), 162, 164.

58. "Tenement House Problem"; "The Tenement Problem."

59. Gompers, *Seventy Years*, 184; "The New Tenement House Act for New York," *Sanitary Engineer* 15 (April 2, 1887); 453–54.

60. The most sophisticated and comprehensive treatment of Henry George and his mayoral campaign is Edward Thomas O'Donnell, *Henry George for Mayor! Irish Nationalism, Labor Radicalism, and Independent Politics in Gilded Age New York*, (forthcoming), esp. chs. 6–7. For an excellent shorter account, see Edwin G. Burrows and Mike Wallace, *Gotham: A History of New York City to 1898* (New York, 1999), 1089–110.

61. Wingate quoted in the *New York Sun*, October 2, 1886, 1; see also coverage in the *New York Times*, October 2, 1886, 1. George quoted in *John Swinton's Paper*, October 10, 1886, 2, which, unlike the New York dailies, provided a full text of George's acceptance speech. See for example the *New York Times*, October 5, 1886, 1. See also John R. Stobo, "Organized Labor, Housing Issues, and Politics: Another Look at the 1886 Henry George Mayoral Campaign in New York City" (MA thesis, Columbia University, 1993).

62. Jacob Riis, "The Tram Strike in New York," *Nationaltidende*, March 5, 1886 (all translations from the Danish by Lone Thygesen Blecher); "Municipal Freshness," *The Standard*, February 5, 1887, Riis Clippings, LC. For background on the Knights of Labor, see Robert E. Weir, *Beyond Labor's Veil: The Culture of the Knights of Labor* (University Park, PA, 1996).

63. "Young Men's Meeting," *Long Island Democrat* (Jamaica), February 1, 1887, Riis Clippings, LC.

64. Jacob Riis, "From New York," *Nationaltidende*, December 17, 1888.

65. Ibid. Jay quoted in "The Religious Needs of the City," *Christian Union* 38 (December 13, 1888), 698. See also coverage of the evangelical conference in the *New York Times*, December 4, 2; December 5, 3; December 6, 2, 1888. Riis discusses the conference's* impact on him in *Making of an American*, 248–49—but as is often the case in the book, he mixes up dates and his memory is confused. The addresses delivered at this conference were later published as Rev. J.M. King et al., *The Religious Condition of New York City* (New York, 1888), but I have used the journalistic accounts for quotations.

66. MacArthur quoted (summarized) in Riis, "From New York," *Nationaltidende*, December 17, 1888; Parkhurst quoted in "The Religious Needs of the City," which also offers a different summary of MacArthur's talk.

67. MacArthur quoted in the *New York Times*, December 5, 1888, 3; "Some Supplementary Remarks," *Christian Union* 38 (December 13, 1888), 681.

68. Riis, *Making of an American*, 265, 266; Helen C. Campbell, *Prisoners of Poverty: Women Wage Earners, Their Trades and Their Lives* (Boston, 1887), i. For a sense of how Riis's breakthrough ratcheted up expectations of and demand for photographs "made from life," see, for example, "Publishers Preface," Helen C. Campbell, Thomas W. Knox, and Thomas Byrnes, *Darkness and Daylight; Lights and Shadows of New York Life: A Pictorial Record of Personal Experiences By Day and Night in the Great Metropolis* (Hartford, 1897), vii–xii.

69. LC Copyright Office title page, March 19, 1888, in General Correspondence, container 4, Riis Papers, LC.

70. *New York Tribune*, January 26, 1888; *New York News*, January 27, 1888; *New York Herald*, January 26, 1888; *New York Tribune*, May 11, 1888, all clippings in "How the Other Half Lives, Lecture Reviews, Serials," container 12, Riis Papers, LC.

71. "The Other Half," *New Bedford Mercury*, May 30, 1888; "New York's Dark Side," *Buffalo Express*, March 26, 1889; A.T. Schauffler to Jacob Riis,

February 29, 1888 (see also, for example, W.T. Elsing, DeWitt Memorial Church, to Jacob Riis, March 12, 1888); Riis quoted in *New York Morning Journal*, February 12, 1888, all clippings in container 12, Riis Papers, LC.

72. For the published version of this lecture, see "The Other Half and How They Live; Story in Pictures," Christians at Work, *Proceedings of Sixth Annual Convention* 6 (1891): 289–311. Hereafter cited as Lecture Transcript. Riis's handwritten note is on his copy of the lecture, in How the Other Half Lives, Book Reviews, Related Material, container 10, Riis Papers, LC.

73. Lecture Transcript, 291, 292, 294; "Slum of a Great City," *Washington Post*, November 10, 1891, clipping in How the Other Half Lives, Book Reviews, Related Material, container 10, Riis Papers, LC.

74. Lecture Transcript, 300, 301, 298.

75. Lecture Transcript, 293, 304, 310–11.

76. Lecture Transcript, 308, 309.

77. Jacob Riis, "The Tenement House Question: I-The Question Stated," and "The Tenement House Question: II-The Remedy," *Christian Union* 39 (May 9, 1889): 590, 591, and (May 16, 1889): 624. See also the related articles, Jacob Riis, "Model Lodgings for the Poor," *Christian Union* 41 (April 3, 1890): 478–79, and "How the Other Half Lives," *Christian Union* 42 (November 27, 1890): 706–7, which includes an interview with Riis and a review of his book.

78. Jacob Riis, "How the Other Half Lives: Studies Among the Tenements," *Scribner's Magazine* 6, December 1889, 643–62. For reviews of this article, see, for example, *New York Evening Post*, December 6, 1889, and *London Morning Advertiser*, December 13, 1889; clippings in How the Other Half Lives, Lecture Reviews, Serials, container 12, Riis Papers, LC; William A. Barnard to Jacob Riis, November 30, 1889, in General Correspondence, container 4, Riis Papers, LC; Scrapbook note in How the Other Half Lives, Book Reviews, Related Material, container 10, Riis Papers, LC.

79. "In the World of Literature," *New York Press*, November 23, 1890; "How the Other Half Lives," *The Independent*, January 1, 1891; clippings in How the Other Half Lives, Book Reviews, Related Material, container 10, Riis Papers, LC. Advertisement for *How the Other Half Lives* in endpapers of Jacob

Riis, *The Children of the Poor* (New York, 1892)—this advertisement first came to my attention in Keith Leland Gandal, "The Spectacle of the Poor: Jacob Riis, Stephen Crane and the Representation of Slum Life" (PhD dissertation, University of California, Berkeley, 1990, 12).

80. Jacob Riis, *How the Other Half Lives: Studies Among the Tenements of New York* (New York, 1890), 2, 3, 162. I have used an 1895 printing (same as first edition) for all quotes.

81. Riis, *How the Other Half Lives*, 1, 7, 19.

82. Riis, *How the Other Half Lives*, 296.

83. Riis, *How the Other Half Lives*, 27, 26, 107, 49.

84. Riis, *How the Other Half Lives*, 27, 95, 96, 102.

85. Riis, *How the Other Half Lives*, 23, 27.

86. Riis, *How the Other Half Lives*, 154, 155, 158, 156.

87. Riis, *How the Other Half Lives*, 80, 243, 246, 181, 185. Riis opened his next book, *The Children of the Poor* (New York, 1892), with the following line: "The problem of the children is the problem of the State. As we mould the children of the toiling masses in our cities, so we shape the destiny of the State which they will rule in their turn, taking the reins from our hands. In proportion as we neglect or pass them by, the blame for bad government to come rests upon us" (1).

88. "Some Supplementary Remarks," *Christian Union* 38 (December 13, 1888): 681; Riis, *How the Other Half Lives*, 5, 271, 284, 283.

89. "How the Other Half Lives," *New York Evening Sun*, November 18, 1890; Alexander L. Kinkhead, "How the Other Half Lives," *The Epoch*, January 16, 1891; "The Seamy Side," *New York Tribune*, November 25, 1890, clippings in How the Other Half Lives, Book Reviews, Related Material, container 10, Riis Papers, LC.

90. Lewis F. Fried, *Makers of the City* (Amherst, 1990), 45. Fried's essay on Riis offers an insightful discussion of the tensions between his rural background and his work in and vision of New York.

91. Jacob Riis to John Riis, July 11, 1904, General Correspondence, container 4, Riis Papers, LC.

92. [E.L. Godkin], "How the Other Half Lives," *New York Evening Post*, February 14, 1891, clipping in How the Other Half Lives, Book Reviews, Related Material, container 10, Riis Papers, LC.

2. Jacob A. Riis, Photographer
"After a Fashion"

1. *The Making of an American* (New York: Macmillan, 1901), 264–71.

2. Beaumont Newhall, *The History of Photography from 1839 to the Present Day* (New York: Museum of Modern Art, 1949), 167–86. In the fifth revised edition of his *History*, Newhall decided that Riis did not warrant this esteemed position and moved the discussion of Riis from the chapter on documentary photography to an earlier chapter, which described turn-of-the-century "journalists, writers, artists, and others who had no desire to take up photography as a profession [but who found] the camera a useful adjunct to their work," and produced "photographs of lasting value." *The History of Photography from 1939 to the Present*, rev. ed. (New York: Museum of Modern Art, 1982), 132.

3. See Bonnie Yochelson, *The Committed Eye: Alexander Alland's Photography* (New York: Museum of the City of New York, 1991).

4. John Szarkowski, *Looking at Photographs* (New York: Museum of Modern Art, 1973), 172. Sally Stein first noted the roles of Alland and Szarkowski in creating "Jacob Riis, modern photographer." See "Making Connections with the Camera, Photography and Social Mobility in the Career of Jacob Riis," *Afterimage*, May 1983, 9–10.

5. The most adamant refutation of Riis's claim is by Peter B. Hales, who asserted that "Riis's bumbling photographer was merely a persona . . . designed to draw the audience's attention away from the manipulations of the creator and the distortions of the medium, to lull viewers into believing themselves witnesses to an unrehearsed and unstaged confrontation with the raw grit of a previously hidden world." See *Silver Cities: The Photography of American Urbanization, 1839–1915* (Philadelphia: Temple University Press, 1984),

193. Following Hales, Colin Westerbrook believed that "the reason [Riis] didn't bother to make his work better was that, as he recognized from the very beginning, a picture made ineptly was more effective for his purposes." See *Bystander: A History of Street Photography* (Boston: Little, Brown, 1994), 241.

6. Alexander Alland, Sr., *Jacob A. Riis, Photographer and Citizen*, (Millerton, NY: Aperture, 1973), 43.

7. *Making of an American*, 203.

8. Ibid., 223.

9. Nagle was head of the Bureau of Vital Statistics in the Health Department. Riis thanked Nagle, "whose friendly camera later on gave me some invaluable lessons." It appears unlikely, however, that Nagle photographed on the midnight excursions, since, in the press notices of Riis's first lecture, only Piffard and Lawrence are credited. *Making of an American*, 243.

10. "Flashes from the Slums," *New York Sun*, February 12, 1888.

11. The Society of Amateur Photographers, [Untitled description of mission, membership, etc.], 1887.

12. In 1891, Alfred Stieglitz joined the society and used it as his base to establish an internationally renowned group of American photographic artists. He quickly assumed a position of leadership in the society, which merged with the Camera Club of New York in 1896. In 1902, Stieglitz left the Camera Club to form his own elite group, the Photo-Secession.

13. Riis collected his press clippings in a scrapbook and titled the pages devoted to his early lectures "Press Comments on the Lecture 'The Other Half, How It Lives and Dies in New York.' " container 12, Jacob A. Riis Papers, Library of Congress. Hereafter cited as Riis Clippings, LC.

14. *New York News*, January 27, 1888, Riis Clippings, LC.

15. *Photographic Times*, February 3, 1888, Riis Clippings, LC.

16. *How the Other Half Lives, Studies Among the Tenements of New York* (New York: Charles Scribner's Sons, 1890).

17. I thank Mary Panzer for alerting me to this practice. That there are no known stereographs from Riis's negatives remains a mystery. When working on her *World History of Photography* (1984), Naomi Rosenblum, however, was

given a 35mm slide of a stereograph of Riis's "Street Arabs in Night Quarters." Neither she nor I have been able to find its source.

18. Maren Stange was the first to explore the relationship between the Richard Hoe Lawrence Collection at the New-York Historical Society and the Jacob A. Riis Collection at the Museum of the City of New York. *Symbols of Ideal Life: Social Documentary Photography in America, 1890–1950* (New York: Cambridge University Press, 1989), 6–12.

19. The society seems to have preferred prints to the original glass slides, which were difficult to store and access. Its photographer did not respect the compositional integrity of the originals and cropped the images, closing in tightly on the figures to heighten the sense of intimacy and drama of the scenes. Alland, who made prints from all of Riis's negatives for the New-York Historical Society in 1950, and John Heffren, who printed Riis negatives for the Museum of the City of New York in 1953, cropped the images for the same reason.

20. In *How the Other Half Lives* (78, 222), Riis described two photographic encounters—one with "The Tramp" and the other with some Hell's Kitchen boys "Showing Their Trick." These photographs were taken with Lawrence and Piffard, but Riis failed to mention them, leading Maren Stange to argue that Riis took credit for work he did not do (*Symbols of Ideal Life*, 9). The argument misconstrues the relationship among the men. Had Riis felt that the role of Lawrence and Piffard was critical, he would have mentioned them, and had they felt wronged they would have protested their omission.

21. *Jamaica Farmer*, February 8, 1888, Riis Clippings, LC.

22. *Making of an American*, 298.

23. "Flashes from the Slums," *New York Sun*, February 12, 1888; and *The Metropolitan*, March 1888, Riis Clippings, LC.

24. A.T. Schauffler, March 3, 1888, letter of recommendation, Container 4, Riis Papers, LC. A review of the Broadway Tabernacle lecture (*New York Evening Post*, February 28, 1888) announces coming engagements at Dr. Kittredge's church at Madison Avenue and 57th Street and [illegible] James Church in Harlem. Neither lecture was given, but on April 26 Riis lectured

at the Lexington Avenue Baptist Church for the benefit of the German Baptist Church in Harlem. Riis Clippings, LC.

25. *Brooklyn Times*, March 8, 1888, Riis Clippings, LC.

26. Amelia B. Sears to Jacob Riis, December 7, 1888, container 4, Riis Clippings, LC; *New Bedford Mercury*, May 3, 1888, Riis Clippings, LC.

27. "The Tenement-House Question: The Question Stated," and "The Tenement-House Question: The Remedy," *Christian Union*, May 1889, container 10, Riis Papers, LC.

28. Only two slides in the Jacob A. Riis Collection, MCNY, bear Lawrence's label; the rest of the slides associated with the first lecture bear Fisk's label. Riis continued to work with Fisk for several years, following him, as he moved from 8 Ann Street to 18 Dey Street to 17 Murray Street; all three addresses appear on slides in the collection. Riis also hired Fisk to work in the field; his name appears on the sleeves of six negatives of photographs that Riis used in 1894 and 1897 articles. In *Jacob A. Riis: Photographer and Citizen* (27), Alland mistakenly identified Fisk as the photographer who tried to cheat Riis by selling prints without Riis's approval.

29. Riis recorded the costs and earnings of his original lecture in the back of an inventory of his negatives that he composed circa 1900.

30. *New York Sun*, February 12, 1888; *New York Morning Journal*, February 12, 1888; *Metropolitan*, March 1888; Riis Clippings, LC. The *Morning Journal* reporter interviewed Riis in his office. The *Sun* reproduced twelve engravings, half of which were borrowed by the *Metropolitan*; Riis lent four other photographs for reproduction to the *Morning Journal*.

31. *Harper's Weekly*, March 10, 1888, cover and 167; *Frank Leslie's Illustrated Weekly*, November 10, 1888, 208.

32. *Making of an American*, 297.

33. "How the Other Half Lives: Studies Among the Tenements," *Scribner's Magazine*, December 1889, 643–62.

34. *Making of an American*, 270.

35. Riis Clippings, LC.

36. "Prayer-Time in the Nursery—Five Points House of Industry," which

appeared as a full-page wood engraving in the article, was reproduced in the book as a full-page halftone.

37. *Making of an American*, 309.

38. *Chicago Tribune*, December 13, 1890, Riis Clippings, LC.

39. *Epoch*, January 16, 1891, Riis Clippings, LC.

40. *Brooklyn Times*, November 29, 1890, Riis Clippings, LC.

41. *Chicago Herald*, January 10, 1891, Riis Clippings, LC.

42. *Critic*, December 29, 1890, Riis Clippings, LC.

43. *Catholic World*, February 1891, Riis Clippings, LC.

44. *Christian Intelligencer*, December 24, 1890, Riis Clippings, LC.

45. *New York Evening Sun*, November 18, 1890, Riis Clippings, LC.

46. *Sunday School Times*, January 17, 1891, Riis Clippings, LC.

47. *Brooklyn Times*, May 9, 1891, Riis Clippings, LC.

48. *Making of an American*, 287–93.

49. The Jacob A. Riis Settlement is currently located in Long Island City, Queens.

50. *Children of the Poor*, (New York: Charles Scribner's Sons, 1892), 1–8.

51. *Children of the Poor*, 60–61.

52. *How the Other Half Lives*, 125–26.

53. Ten of the article's fourteen illustrations were based on Riis's photographs. The remaining four consisted of three original drawings by the primary copyist Victor Perard and an engraving after a portrait of Charles Loring Brace, founder of the Children's Aid Society.

54. Of the twenty-four new illustrations, half were from Riis photos, seven from artists' drawings, and five from photos that Riis had acquired from other sources.

55. *Brooklyn Times*, November 12, 1892, Riis Clippings, LC.

56. *Making of an American*, 309.

57. *Charities Review*, January 1893, Riis Clippings, LC.

58. *Christian Register*, December 1, 1892, Riis Clippings, LC.

59. *New York Tribune*, November 20, 1892, Riis Clippings, LC.

60. *Nibsy's Christmas* (1893; repr., Freeport, NY: Books for Libraries Press, 1969).

61. The negatives, lantern slides, and vintage prints in the Jacob A. Riis Collection, MCNY, represent 559 images. Of these, 250 were taken by Riis or commissioned by him and 309 are copies of prints that Riis acquired from a variety of sources. Of the 250 images, 57 were by Lawrence and Piffard, 9 were by Collins, and 12 were by Fisk. (Two 5 x 7 inch negatives were made for a 1892 *Evening Sun* article by an unidentified photographer.) Riis took 53 of the new images published in *How the Other Half Lives* and *Children of the Poor*. He took 75 new images, which appeared in newspapers and magazines articles between 1889 and 1898. There are 42 Riis images that were not published, and of those 21 cannot be dated.

62. *New York Evening Sun*, July 25, 1889, Riis Clippings, LC. The article also included an image of residents of Blindman's Alley by Piffard and Lawrence.

63. *New York Evening Sun*, April 28, 1891, Riis Clippings, LC. Four negatives of Smallpox Island, also called North Brother Island, belong to the Riis Collection, MCNY.

64. *New York Evening Sun*, June 6, 1891, Riis Clippings, LC. The negatives for three of the five images reproduced are in the Riis Collection, MCNY.

65. *Making of an American,* 228–30; and "Some Things We Drink," *Evening Sun*, August 21, 1891, Riis Clippings, LC. Six months earlier on February 10, 1891, Riis wrote an exposé for the *Evening Sun* about sewer refuse running directly into an old water tank in lower Manhattan. Accompanying officers of the Board of Health who sought a water sample, Riis took his camera but found the conditions too daunting to photograph; the article was illustrated instead with line drawings.

66. There are no extant negatives for these images; they are known only through the eleven prints that Riis pasted in his clippings scrapbook, Riis Clippings, LC.

67. The Riis Collection, MCNY, includes nine images from the dump series, five of which were included in "Wharf Rats." Several negatives, including "A Child of the Dump," have been lost, and three were never published.

68. "Police Lodging-Houses: Are They Hotbeds for Typhus Fever?" *Christian Union*, January 14, 1893, Riis Clippings, LC.

69. "Vice Which is Unchecked," *New York Tribune*, January 31, 1892; "Foul Lodging Rooms," *New York Evening Sun*, February 17, 1893; "Police Lodging-Houses"; "Police Lodgings," *World, Brooklyn Edition*, February 12, 1893; notice for presentation at New-York Academy of Medicine, February 1, 1893, Riis Clippings, LC.

70. In the *World*, Riis mentioned that typhus had appeared in the Oak Street and Madison Street stations; on the negative sleeve for a photograph of the East 22nd Street station, he remarked, "where typhus came." The Charity Organization Society initiative is discussed in "A Municipal Lodging House," *New York Tribune*, March 2, 1893, Riis Clippings, LC.

71. It also became the centerpiece of a chapter in his autobiography. "My Dog Is Avenged," *Making of an American*, 235–62.

72. "Police Lodging-Houses," 84.

73. This is the only image that can definitely be dated to the winter of 1893; the rest were taken in either 1892 or 1893.

74. *Century Magazine*, September 1894, 657–66. Riis exposed seven negatives for this series, two of which were published.

75. *Century Magazine*, November 1894, 109–16. Riis exposed four negatives of the Juvenile Asylum, none of which were used for the article.

76. Fisk's staged scenes depict the "problem"—boys shooting craps on a street corner—and Riis's "solution"—"The Mulberry Street Drill Gang," which shows boys organized into a marching club. Unlike Riis, who usually exposed one negative for each scene he photographed, Fisk worked more professionally, exposing four negatives for "Shooting Craps" and two for "Drilling the Gang."

77. *Century Magazine*, December 1894, 303–308. Although the article was not published until 1895, the negative sleeves noted that the photographs were taken in October 1894. The article included four of Riis's eight images.

78. *Making of an American*, 274.

79. "Goodby to the Bend," *Evening Sun*, May 25, 1895, Riis Clippings, LC.

80. The location where Riis took these photographs remains unclear. Although he published the photograph of a baby in a dark tenement hall under several titles, none mentions location. The midnight lodgers' negative sleeve reads, "Midnight at Bayard Street," but in *The Battle with the Slum*, the image is captioned, "Night in Gotham Court," which is not in the Bend.

81. Riis wrote, "Taken by Mr. Collins of Eve. Sun" on the sleeves of eleven negatives, which he kept in sequence.

82. *Review of Reviews*, August 1895, 172–78.

83. These before-and-after photographs first appeared in "A New Broom on New York Streets: Results of Colonel Waring's Work Contrasted with the Results of Tammany, from Photographs of the Same Localities Taken in 1893 and 1895," *Harper's Weekly*, June 22, 1895. In *Garbage! The History and Politics of Trash in New York City* (New York Public Library, 1994), Elizabeth Fee and Steven H. Corey mistakenly attribute these photographs to Riis because they encountered Riis's copy negatives in the Riis Collection, MCNY.

84. Four of these photographs were used in "Where Santa Claus Will Not Go," a typical Christmas season article that appeared in the *Journal*, December 22, 1895, Riis Clippings LC.

85. *New York Evening Sun*, April 16, 1897, Riis Clippings, LC.

86. *Century Magazine*, "The Passing of Cat Alley," December 1898, 156–76.

87. The claim was incorrect: of the article's eight illustrations, two had been previously published, two were by Fisk, and only four were new.

88. *New York Journal*, December 22, 1895, Riis Clippings, LC.

89. The Museum of the City of New York holds eighty-three slides of public baths by Stopft.

90. The client(s) for these photographs in the Byron Collection, Museum of the City of New York, is unknown. Of the fifteen photographs dated 1896 and 1897, three depict tenement families in their homes; seven are staged genre scenes in a tenement setting; and five show poor people in a studio setting, posed against a plain backdrop.

91. *Children of the Tenements* (1903; repr. Freeport, NY: Short Story Index Reprint Series, Books for Libraries Press, 1970).

92. *The Ten Years' War: An Account of the Battle with the Slum in New York* (1900, repr., Freeport, NY: Books for Libraries Press, 1969), 127.

93. See Stange, *Symbols of Ideal Life*, 28–46, for an extensive discussion of the exhibition.

94. "The Tenement House Exhibition," *Harper's Weekly*, February 3, 1900, 104.

95. Ibid., and "The New York Tenement-House Commission," *Review of Reviews*, January 1900, 689–96.

96. The COS gave these panels to the Museum of the City of New York. They are stamped on the back "Tenement House Committee." One of the panels, which is made from a different color board and is written in a different hand, bears the notation "Tenement House Department"; it was probably added shortly after the department was formed in 1901.

97. The negative sleeves are often marked "Organized Charity," which stands for Charity Organization Society.

98. The copy negatives are $3\frac{1}{4} \times 4\frac{1}{4}$ inches, smaller than Riis's 4 x 5–inch negatives. Many of the later lantern slides bear the name William T. Gregg or Charles Besseler, the commercial photographers who made the slides and may have made the copy negatives.

99. The inventory was part of the gift of the Jacob A. Riis Collection to the Museum of the City of New York. Approximately 150 negatives of the Riis family at home and in Denmark are missing; it is most likely that Roger William Riis removed these negatives when he donated the collection. There are approximately 25 other negatives missing—broken or lost by Riis—most of which exist in lantern slide form.

100. Riis published one of the images—"Tramps Lodging in a Jersey Street Yard"—in an article, "Battle with the Slum," *Churchman* 24, October 12, 1901, 482, which came out at about the same time.

101. Riis discussed but did not reproduce "The Survival of the Unfittest" in *Children of the Poor* (13). On its negative sleeve, he explained the sig-

nificance of the image: "rear tenement disclosed, buried in business houses, in middle of block, by the building of an addition to the Puck Building in Mulberry St." That addition was constructed in 1892, the same year that *Children of the Poor* was published. The "Jersey Street Yard," on nearby Jersey Street between Mulberry and Crosby Streets, was probably taken around the same time. The lantern slide for the image was made by A.D. Fisk, the professional photographer who made Riis's other slides in 1892. Writing in 1900, Riis noted on the image's negative sleeve: "Yard in Jersey Street (now gone) where Italians lived in the then worst slums."

102. Two other images—of "A Cellar Dive in the Bend" and "A Seven Cent Lodging House"—were taken by Lawrence and Piffard. The fifth "new" image, "The Slide That Was the Children's Only Playground Once," shows a merchant's cellar door spiked with nails to prevent children from playing on it.

103. "The Golden Rule in Poverty Row," September 27, 1905, 795ff; "The Gateway of All Nations," October 11, 1905, 843ff; "The Children of the Darkness and the Important Part that We May Play in Bringing Them into the Light," March [illegible], 1906, 249f.

104. "What One Wild Flower Did," December 1907, 230–32; "Our Roof Garden Among the Tenements," December 1908, 216–17. The photographs in the first article were by Leonard Barron and C.E. Batcheller, and in the second by Alice Boughton and Henry H. Saylor.

105. Jacob A. Riis to Miss Waterbury, June 30, 1909, Jacob Riis Settlement Papers, box 8, folder 6, New York Public Library.

106. For a fuller discussion of this book, see Hales, *Silver Cities*, 233–42.

107. See Hales, *Silver Cities*, 221–22.

108. My thanks to Jack Judson, Director of the Magic Lantern Castle Museum, San Antonio, Texas, for alerting me to this catalog in his collection.

109. Alland, *Jacob A. Riis: Photographer and Citizen* 11.

110. See Lewis F. Fried, "Jacob A. Riis: The City as Christian Fraternity," in *Makers of the City* (University of Massachusetts Press, 1990), 10–63.

111. J. Riis Owre, epilogue to *The Making of an American by Jacob A. Riis* (London: Macmillan, 1970), 292–93, 332–33.

Index

Note: Page numbers in *italics* indicate photographs and illustrations.